My SPIRITUAL JOURNEY *into* CHRIST CONSCIOUSNESS

GILBERT ANDRES ESQUIBEL

BALBOA.
PRESS
A DIVISION OF HAY HOUSE

Balboa Press books may be ordered through booksellers or by contacting:

Balboa Press
A Division of Hay House
1663 Liberty Drive
Bloomington, IN 47403
www.balboapress.com
1 (877) 407-4847

Because of the dynamic nature of the Internet, any web addresses or links contained in this book may have changed since publication and may no longer be valid. The views expressed in this work are solely those of the author and do not necessarily reflect the views of the publisher, and the publisher hereby disclaims any responsibility for them.

The author of this book does not dispense medical advice or prescribe the use of any technique as a form of treatment for physical, emotional, or medical problems without the advice of a physician, either directly or indirectly. The intent of the author is only to offer information of a general nature to help you in your quest for emotional and spiritual well-being. In the event you use any of the information in this book for yourself, which is your constitutional right, the author and the publisher assume no responsibility for your actions.

Any people depicted in stock imagery provided by Thinkstock are models, and such images are being used for illustrative purposes only.
Certain stock imagery © Thinkstock.

Print information available on the last page.

ISBN: 978-1-5043-3521-8 (sc)
ISBN: 978-1-5043-3523-2 (hc)
ISBN: 978-1-5043-3522-5 (e)

Library of Congress Control Number: 2015910988

Balboa Press rev. date: 11/4/2015

This book is dedicated to
My brother and friend
Jeshua,
Who has guided my
Life from the beginning of my
Spiritual journey

I also dedicate this book
To my late soul mate Linda,
Who has had and continues
To have a great influence
In my life.

I also want to express my deepest gratitude
To my best friend Ashley who gave me
Great encouragement and support
During my writing of this book
And was instrumental in the editing of this book

CONTENTS

FOREWORD

I have written this book to reach those light workers who are still asleep and for others who really want to know what our life here on earth is about and therefore I will touch on many different levels of truths. As some of you already know, when a person reaches a state of full spiritual awakening, he or she will be totally aware that the world we seem to live in and the entire physical universe is one very vivid dream and in reality never did exist. Everything that ever seemed to happen, everything that seems to be happening now, or will happen in the future in the physical universe, in fact never happened. The question is, how far down the rabbit hole are we willing to go?

Yet there is another part to this conundrum of living in this dream world, which is that there is a powerful cosmic purpose for going through this illusion. The purpose of going through this illusion is so profound and meaningful that when understood, it will shatter all belief in judgment and guilt. Those who have voluntarily chosen to enter the darkness and illusion of this world are very brave and bold adventurers. The contribution they are making to the expansion of creation and to the nature of God is unprecedented and priceless. This concept may be hard to accept for most people. Even some on the spiritual path may have a hard time accepting it, but it is a truth which Jeshua has spoken about and which I will expound upon in this book.

Please note that throughout this book I will use the name Jeshua instead of Jesus because this was his name when he walked the earth. Another reason for using the name Jeshua instead of Jesus is that the name Jesus has been so misrepresented in religious doctrine that much of the pure truth which he brought into the earth has been lost in the dogma of religion. Let me also add that Jeshua does not in any way desire to be worshiped or looked on as someone superior. He wants to be seen as our brother and friend.

We have so many concepts, opinions, desires, beliefs and identifications that keep the truth buried deep within our minds. Stripping away these false beliefs and identifications so that we can realize who we are is what Jeshua meant when he said that a person must give up his life to find life. When that which is false is eliminated, the truth will shine forth revealing that everything that seemed to take place in this world, took place in an illusory dream of duality. There is no need to feel guilty about anything.

When we reach a state of realizing the real purpose of our journey on earth, the concept of judging others will completely disappear. We are all perfectly innocent, we always have been and always will be. The intellectual mind and individuality will not be able to comprehend this truth because the limited mind perceives things through the filter of limitation, judgment and separation and cannot conceive of infinity and oneness.

The intent of this book is to help awaken the state of innocence and oneness in all who seek it. Accepting Our Innocence is a very necessary step on the path to our awakening. It is not something we have to earn, it is our birthright. It is our very nature. The unbalanced ego, which you will read about in this book, will do everything in its power to keep us from accepting our innocence. Please note that any reference to the ego in this book will be referring to the unbalanced ego unless noted otherwise. The pure ego in itself is a positive and necessary aspect of who we are. It is when it becomes unbalanced and takes over our lives, that it becomes a destructive force. We all have the ability to bring our egos back into balance so that we can become a great light for others. Our spiritual journey will ultimately lead us on a path in which we will perceive both the light and dark elements of life as two halves of a whole and we will transcend the idea of duality.

We gave the ego the power to take over our lives when we first began this journey into illusion. When we are ready, we begin the process of bringing it back into balance. This is not an easy task and many of the people on earth are not at a stage of spiritual development which would make it feasible to even begin this process. There is no judgment or sense of comparison in this statement. It simple reflects the current conditions here on earth at this time.

Beyond this world of illusion there is an Existence, which is so much greater than our wildest dreams here on earth. The greatest goal, and the only true goal, is for a person to heal themselves and discover who he or she truly is. This discovery will lead us face to face with the knowing that we are one with God. We are greater than we can ever even begin to imagine with our intellect, because our intellect cannot imagine such greatness. Never the less, this is who we are. The ultimate destiny of all who have ever walked the earth is to realize and experience our oneness with God. I hope my message, through this book, will be a light on the path for all who read it.

There may be new concepts for some reading this book so I have used many analogies and stories in writing this book so the reader can more easily grasp the essence of what is being written. The Teacher who taught me and prepared me is not of this world. This Teacher, Who is in all of us, is just waiting for us to make the decision to know the truth. The Teacher I am referring to is the Holy Spirit. The Holy Spirit has nothing to do with Christianity or religion. The term Holy Spirit is also known as the Inner Self or Divine Consciousness. Any true spiritual master is part of the mind of the Holy Spirit. The Holy Spirit is that part of our mind which we share with God. The Holy Spirit is buried deeply in the minds of many people but can never be lost completely. When we are ready, She simply allows us to remember what we have forgotten, which is our perfection and oneness with God.

I have used 'him' and 'her' interchangeably in this book. When we reach our final destination we will find that male and female do not exist in the way we think about it here on earth. When a person reaches a certain state of spiritual realization, she will realize that each one of us contain both the male and female aspects in perfect balance. Throughout this book I have occasionally interspersed a question and answer format in anticipation to questions which I felt would be in the minds of many of the readers.

For the past twenty years I have been having very deep profound spiritual experiences. Shortly after I started having these experiences I began reading a book entitled 'A Course in Miracles'. It was very interesting to see that many of the spiritual experiences and realizations I was experiencing were expounded upon in the teachings of A Course in Miracles. I would highly recommend that any sincere seeker read and reread A Course in Miracles. This book was dictated by Jeshua to a woman named Helen Schucman over a period of seven years beginning in 1965. A Course in Miracles expresses the Truth with a clarity which can help any spiritual aspirant on their spiritual journey. There are many paths that lead to spiritual enlightenment. I am not implying that A Course in Miracles contains the total picture of our spiritual journey. It does give a sincere spiritual devotee the tools which will allow her to let go of illusion, so that the way is made clear for a spiritual rebirth. Rebirth means a total change in consciousness and perception of how we see ourselves, others and the world. When a soul reaches a certain level of spiritual development, he will be able to live in the world without any judgment or attachment to the things of the world. He will be in the world, but not of it.

My spiritual journey was a very long and difficult one. I always believed that I would reach my spiritual destination, but there were many, many times that my path seemed very dark and hopeless. I went through periods of questioning whether my goal was just a fantasy in my mind. None of us will travel the same path. For some the road will be much smoother than for others, but there is one thing that all who have reached the 'Promised Land' will have in common. Each one that reaches this state of consciousness will have voluntarily relinquished their own personal ego, which consists of the identification and attachment to the limited and flawed individual we believe we are. When you complete this book I hope you will have a much greater understanding of what the ego is, because it is always best to understand your adversary which is doing everything in its' power to keep you asleep in illusion.

Our scientific discoveries in the field of quantum physics are now doing more than many religions to help mankind find the truth. Quantum physicists have discovered that what appears to be the concrete world is really all happening in our mind. In other words, the world we seem to live in is not real. It is a figment of our imagination. Albert Einstein summed this idea up in his statement, "Reality is merely an illusion, albeit a very persistent one." Science will never be able to fully reveal what the truth is, but quantum physics is helping people release their concepts of what we consider to be the concrete world and thus helping people to prepare themselves for a deeper understanding of reality. Letting go of false concepts is a necessary part in remembering what is real.

Another revealing finding in quantum physics is that each one of us is responsible for creating our own reality through our beliefs, choices, desires, thoughts and emotions. Quantum physicists have also discovered that time is not linear and that on the quantum level a person could just as easily go backward or forward in time. An amazing world of possibilities has been revealed through quantum physics, but it is our spiritual development which will bring all of this into total clarity and understanding. Spiritual awakening brings about the realization that God and you are one.

We all have the memory of the whole truth within us. Trust that the truth within you will lead you home. Jeshua said, "You shall know the truth and the truth shall set you free." As the truth of who we are begins to dawn in our minds, we realize that we have the power within us to totally transform our minds and lives completely. It is up to us.

Be patient with yourself for I can assure you that if you are sincere about remembering who you are, you are headed for the most glorious destination imaginable. I am not saying the spiritual path will be a bed of roses, because the spiritual path requires that each of us must voluntarily surrender the illusionary, separated identity we believe we are. The spiritual journey will eventually lead to our own personal crucifixion of our ego. Don't be concerned about whether you are ready to walk the spiritual path, because we are never given anything we are not ready to handle. Be persistent in your striving for spiritual realization and you will be blessed with all that is needed to reach your destination.

CHAPTER 1

Spiritual Realizations

Before I tell you a little about my journey in life, I want to clarify one very important truth which goes to the foundation of spiritual understanding. Most people believe in a God who judges and determines what is going to happen in a person's life. This is totally false. We and we alone determine what happens in our lives by our beliefs and actions. When a soul reaches a certain level of spiritual development, he will realize that he is God on earth. At the very core of our being, each and every one of us is a very unique part of God. Each one of us carries a unique sound, color, frequency and light of God which makes us unique from every other soul ever created. And yet in this uniqueness we are all one in God. A sincere seeker will eventually come to this realization. This truth puts the full responsibility on all that happens to us in our own hands. We and we alone are a law unto our self and in this understanding and application we have great responsibility and the key to our spiritual freedom.

My personal journey in this lifetime was definitely not a bed of roses as I suffered deeply on so many levels. I was born on November 19, 1941 in the mountains of New Mexico in a little town called Park View. I was born into a very large family, thirteen children. I do not remember much about the first four years of my life except that I had the feeling at the age of three or four that I could do anything. I was a very bold and confident child. In those early years I also had the sense that I had to be perfect. If I thought I made a mistake of any kind, I would get very embarrassed. One example was when I was three years old I wet my pants and I was so embarrassed that I hid for the whole day. My family was looking for me everywhere but could not find me. Finally I came out and confessed to my mom what had happened. Of course it is very normal for a three year old to wet their pants, but somehow I had the attitude that I was not supposed to have any of the human shortcomings and because of this I caused myself much unnecessary suffering the majority of my life. I mentally and emotionally beat myself up as my defects became more and more apparent. This need to be perfect followed me a good portion of my life until I realized the foolishness of this striving. I have since understood that my striving for perfection is an illusion because we are always expanding and gaining new experiences, as is God, for we are One.

Our family was poor but I think the early years of my life were mainly happy. My life changed drastically when I was four years old. My mom died shortly after giving birth to her thirteenth child, my youngest sister. It was at this time that my whole world was turned upside down. A few days before her death, my dad took my younger brother and me to New Mexico to stay with relatives in order to give my mom a chance to rest and recuperate after having given birth. My dad got a phone call a couple of days later informing him that mom had been taken to the hospital and he flew back to California to be with her. She passed on before he got there. My younger brother and I never even got a chance to go to the funeral. We were immediately sent to an orphanage for boys in Albuquerque. The orphanage was run by Catholic nuns. Many of the nuns in the orphanage were very cruel and some were even sadistic. The nun who was directly in charge of us was particularly sadistic and for some reason seemed to single me out for blame when something went wrong.

The loss of my mom, dad, and family at that young age really stunted my emotional development. The punishments and beatings handed out by the nuns and their doctrine of sin and guilt, which were daily drummed into our heads, did not help the situation. The orphanage was definitely not a place for a child to develop a healthy emotional system. The death of my mom and my experience in the orphanage left me a very emotionally and mentally confused, angry young boy. After five years in the orphanage, my dad was finally able to bring us home from the orphanage. By that time I had erected an impenetrable protective shield around myself and as a result I had a hard time bonding with my dad and siblings.

Before I had fully erected the protective shield around myself, I was given a glimpse of who I am. In the orphanage, we were not allowed to have any money. If a relative happened to send a child some money, the nuns would intercept it and keep it. One day on the playground I was with my brother and a friend and out of the clear, I said that I was going to find some money. I then pointed to a spot on the ground and said, "There is a dime." I swept back the dirt from that spot and there was a dime. I then walked over to another spot and said, "There is a quarter." I again swept back the dirt and there was a quarter. I did this about 10 or 15 times and each time there was the exact coin denomination at the exact spot where I said it would be. At the time I was either 5 or 6 years old and didn't think much about it. It seemed natural to me that the coins should be where I said they would be. It wasn't till much later that I realized what had actually happened.

I do not feel any judgment towards anyone regarding my experience in the orphanage because I know that before I came into this earth, I chose to go through these experiences for a personal spiritual reason. When we understand that we and we alone create, or choose, our own reality, it will be much easier to let go of all anger and judgments.

As I grew older my insecurity and anger prevented me from really opening up to anybody. Even though I had friends, I usually had a feeling of being isolated, of not fitting in. Even the girlfriends I had were unable to penetrate my defenses. The only time I felt like I belonged was when I was playing sports because I usually did well in athletics and sports did not require intimate communication. Because the military draft was in effect at that time, I joined the army right after high school and spent three years in the military in Japan.

I got out of the army in the spring of 1962. For the next six years I was pretty much caught up in the illusions of this world. Like most people, I was trying to make as much money as I could and was always looking for that perfect girl who would make my life complete. During three of those years I was heavily involved in gambling by playing the horses and cards.

In 1967 my younger brother introduced me to marijuana and a little latter on to LSD. I resisted at first, but because some of my friends were willing to take the plunge, I tried it also. The effect of these drugs was to awaken a very strong longing for God deep inside myself, which caused me to totally reevaluate my life. Let me be very clear that I do not recommend drugs as a way to accelerate a person's spiritual growth. Drugs simply helped to awaken my strong yearning for God. The journey I experienced of preparing myself for spiritual realization was a very long and difficult process. Fortunately, in this day and age the spiritual path is much easier to find and walk. Each of us has a very unique path to travel and if we are sincere about enlightenment, everything we need will be provided.

Shortly after my exposure to drugs, I quit the job I had at Raytheon Electronics and pretty much dropped out of society, as the term was used back in the 1960's. For the next two years I became more and more of a loner because the outer world no longer held much of an attraction for me. While my friends continued to party, I spent most of the time alone contemplating the reality of God and my relationship to Him. During parts of those two years I lived in my station wagon while I tried to understand the purpose of my life. I devoured every spiritual book I could get my hands on. I was, at that time, especially drawn to the metaphysical information which came through the readings given by Edgar Cayce. I even gave lectures at the high school I had attended, on the spiritual information that came through the readings of Edgar Cayce.

In 1969 the direction of my life changed dramatically because of an experience I had. On a very beautiful spring day I drove up to some hills in northern California to get away from the city and to contemplate my new direction in life. I climbed up to the top of one of the hills and laid down under a tree besides a stream. I was looking up at the sky when all of a sudden a huge vision of Jeshua appeared above me. His arms were to the side with his palms opened. I felt myself leave my body and float up to where Jeshua was and we began to talk. I am not conscious of what was said, except for a comment which he made about my body. When he said this, I looked down and saw my body lying beneath the tree. I don't know how long our conversation lasted before I floated back into my body. When I entered my body a question immediately arose in my mind: "What is God?" The answer from within was immediate and the voice I heard was the most beautiful yet authoritative I had ever heard: **"Mind in Space."** I will never forget that voice or those words. After a short time I got up and started walking on one of the many paths that marked the hill. As I walked I heard the same inner voice talking to me about the spiritual path. In essence, the voice told me that I would encounter many things on my spiritual journey that would appear to be good and right, but to remain simple and I would reach my destination.

Shortly after that experience I came to the conclusion that I was on earth for a purpose and that I had better get back into the flow of life until that purpose was revealed to me. I signed up to go to college in the summer of 1969. Two weeks before my first day of college I received a pamphlet in the mail from somebody who attended the same high school I did. I did not know the person who sent it very well and so it was interesting that he would send it to me. I don't even know how he got my mailing address. The pamphlet was about a spiritual group called the Holy Order of MANS. There were also many women in the Order as the term MANS is an acronym for the striving of the members. The Order was started through a revelation from Jeshua to the head of the Order, Father Paul, who was a very highly evolved spiritual master. The main headquarters of the Order was in San Francisco, about 20 minutes from where I was living at the time. The pamphlet intrigued me because the Order's teachings were not based on Western religious doctrine, but had more of an eastern mystical and metaphysical flavor. I wanted to find out more about this Order, so a few days before I was to start college I decided to take a drive to San Francisco and talk to somebody from the Order to find out more about this organization and their purpose.

When I arrived at the main Order house, a priest was summoned to talk to me about their purpose and to answer any questions I had. While talking to the priest I intuitively knew that this was where I was supposed to be at that time. While the priest was speaking to me, my mind came up with many reasons why I could not join the Order, but intuitively I knew my rationalizations would be of no avail. I knew this was where I was supposed to be at that time. I moved into the Holy Order of Mans' main house in San Francisco that very day. It was an abrupt and total severing of my old way of life.

On my first day in the Order I received a message from Jeshua. He told me to be at peace with myself and to know that the Christ life would manifest in me. These words gave me hope as I endured my first year in the Order which was pure hell. The ego was in full battle mode and did everything in its power to get me to leave. I told a friend, after my first year in the Order, that I would not go through that year again even if they offered me a billion dollars and I was very, very serious. It was that difficult because of the mental, emotional and physical discomfort I was experiencing. During that first year, the back of my head, right about where the medulla oblongata is located, felt like it was constantly burning, as if a piece of hot coal was placed there. The top of my head where the crown chakra is located was also continually very hot and uncomfortable. Another interesting physical experience that I had during my first year in the Order was that the soft spot on the top of my head opened up just as it had been when I was a baby. It stayed opened for a few months.

After two years in the Order, I was ordained a priest on July the 4th, 1971. Unfortunately the insecurity and anger that had plagued me most of my life was still a constant companion. Even though I was with men and women of like mind in the Order, I still could not open up and bond with others. I did a lot of teaching and counseling as a priest, but I did not feel the peace and love which I knew were needed to be a true spiritual teacher.

After nine years I left the Order. About a month before I left the Order, I had a very vivid dream in which Jeshua appeared to me and told me he was going to place me on a different path. I was in Boston at the time and the thought of leaving the Order had not previously crossed my mind. A month after the dream I appeared before the Order council and requested a sabbatical. After a year away from the Order I felt no inner urging to return so I wrote the council informing them of my resignation. I had the good fortune of meeting some very highly spiritually evolved men and women in the Order and went through a purification process that was invaluable. Probably one of the most important things that I learned during my time in the Order was how to still my mind through a great deal of concentration exercises and to be aware that I was the observer of my thoughts and not the thinker. I will always be very grateful for the spiritual progress I experienced while I was in the Holy Order of MANS.

After leaving the Order, I stayed in Boston for a year to work and save some money. A year later, I left Boston and moved to Marin County in California. One year later I met a soul mate who would have a big impact in my life. Her name was Linda and I met her at a spiritual lecture in Marin. She intuitively immediately recognized me as I walked into the hall and approached me after the lecture. We talked as if we had known each other for years. I was with her for almost 29 years before her sudden and totally unexpected departure from this earth on May 2, 2010. I will speak more about the impact that her departure had on my life later in the book. When I met her, she was very involved in a spiritual group called Siddha Yoga and for the next 15 years I too became very involved with this group. Then one day the realization came to me that it was time for me to continue my spiritual development on my own, without the help of a physical teacher. I had received a great deal of grace during my time with the Holy Order of MANS and Siddha Yoga, but it was now time to fully accept the reality of what I had been taught for over 26 years. My inner self was apparently notifying me that I no longer needed a physical teacher for this final step.

It was during this period of my life that I began to have some of my most profound spiritual experiences. I had many meditation experiences during this time in which I experienced without a doubt, the absolute truth that I was one with God, pure and perfect in every way without any loss of individuality. In this sacred union there was still relationship. It was not only a realization of who I was, but an experience of a state of being. Many times I experienced the state of being a Christed being, totally pure and holy. These experiences were so sacred and beautiful, it would be impossible to fully describe them in words. During these meditations there was white light all around me. During one of these meditations I experienced the decent of the Holy Spirit into me in the form of a ball of white light. As I was having this experience I was prompted by the spirit to say out loud, "The decent of the Holy Spirit." Initially I didn't say anything and I was again prompted to say it out loud. I feel that the purpose of having me say this out loud was to impress in my mind the importance of this experience. During my meditations I had many experiences which revealed to me very clearly that our separation from God never really occurred and that the separation was in fact impossible. The first time I experienced this, I had to start laughing at the absurdity of our belief in this world as being real. During some of these meditations I actually stepped outside the illusion of time and space and experienced its unreality in a way that was so clear and comprehensible, that my perception of the world completely changed. These spiritual experiences opened my consciousness to a completely new way of perceiving the world and how I experienced my own self. I am forever grateful to Jeshua for his guidance throughout my spiritual journey.

I want to also share a meditation experience I had shortly before sending this book to the publisher. In meditation I was shown very clearly that every cell in my body was in the process of being transformed into God Consciousness. I not only saw this, I experienced the feeling of my cells going through this metamorphosis. Earlier I had been told that the God Gene had exploded in me which seemed to be confirmed through this meditation. I'm not sure how long this process will take before coming into full manifestation.

As a side note, I would like to share an experience that happened to me around the year 2000. I was working in San Francisco at that time and I would normally take the bus to work each day, but on this particular day I drove to work because I had to leave early. I left work in the early afternoon that day. It had rained in the morning and as I was driving across the Golden Gate Bridge, back to our house in Marin County, I saw a beautiful rainbow in the sky. One end of the rainbow appeared to be at the very end of the bridge. As you all know, when we move towards a rainbow it continually recedes so that we can never come in contact with it. As I continued to drive towards the end of the rainbow it did not appear to move. I was very surprised that it seemed to be stationary. I continued moving towards it until I passed right through the end of the rainbow in my car. I was very amazed. I feel that experiences like that were symbolic of the great blessings that lay in store for me.

CHAPTER 2

The Search for Truth

Our search for truth is a journey of self-understanding and realization. When we complete our journey on this level of existence, we will have realized our oneness with God. There are generally four stages which a soul will pass through as she begins her search for God. These four stages may not happen in distinct chronological order as some will blend with others as a person progresses on the spiritual path. Some may not go through this process at all, as there are some who have awakened without ever consciously seeking in this lifetime. There are also some who may awaken before they are even ready for the experience. It would be like a flower bud which opens too early in the season and then is lost when a late freeze occurs. There are also many levels at which a soul may awaken, but for now let's look at these four stages.

The first stage of awakening has to do with disillusionment. This is the beginning stage in which a soul realizes that his current life is not fulfilling and there is a desire for something else. He may not know at this time exactly what he is looking for, but his desire for change will lead him to circumstances which will open his mind to a new way of thinking.

I entered the first stage of my spiritual journey in1968. I had a good job and a comfortable life but at some point I realized that what I was doing was not truly satisfying. I knew there was more to life than going to work, earning a living and partying on the weekends. There was a strong yearning in me to know the deeper truths of life. Who are we, what are we doing here and what happens to us after our bodies stop breathing? During this time I used to go to a small park near my apartment and sit under a big weeping willow tree and contemplate these metaphysical questions for hours. These questions led me to read many spiritual books. As I mentioned earlier, I was especially drawn at that time to reading about the life of Edgar Cayce. Cayce was called 'The Sleeping Prophet'. Cayce found out as a very young man he had the ability to put himself into a self-induced trance which gave him full access to the akashic records which are the records of everything that ever happened on this earth as well as future events which are likely to happen. With free will, man can always change the course of destiny so the future is never absolute. While in this trance, he was asked many questions. In the beginning the questions mainly dealt with health issues. The answers that Cayce gave to these questions usually brought up past life issues which were, in many cases, influencing the current health conditions of the questioner. But what fascinated me the most were answers Cayce gave in response to questions about God and the journey of the souls. The understanding I gleaned from those metaphysical answers awakened a vague remembrance deep within me that I was much more than the individual I had identified with all my life. I realized at that time that I could never go back to the old life I had been living. It was at that time that my spiritual journey, in this life, began in earnest. I had entered stage one of my journey back home. Stage one can manifest as many changes in a person's life. My circle of friends dwindled as I spent much more time alone. Stage one is usually not a lengthy time period, because once a soul fully realizes that the road she has been traveling is not taking her where she wants to go, there should be no reason to continue on that path. Fear of change is what holds some back from beginning this amazing journey.

Stage two of the spiritual journey consists of self-awareness. A person starts becoming more aware of his thought patterns and belief systems which have been leading him down a path of futility. He recognizes, through introspection, that his choices and direction in life had pretty much gone unquestioned until this point. During this stage, a soul will start to make changes to the way he thinks and what he believes about life. This is a period in which a person starts to realize that the ego has been controlling his life and causing him many problems. The task during this phase is to begin making efforts to let go of the ego patterns. One day during this second stage, I was sitting at home with my brother and a couple of friends when a deep realization of the illusion of this life dawned in my mind. Out loud I said, "Who am I? I know I am called Gil but this is not who I am." This was the beginning of the unravelling of who I thought I was and the slow process of becoming who I really am. The door had now been opened to the long difficult journey towards Christ Consciousness.

When I entered this stage back in 1968, all my old belief systems came under scrutiny and I began to make many changes to the way I thought and acted. As I mentioned earlier, I spent a great deal of time alone as I made the effort to change the direction of my life. Gaining spiritual understanding is a big part of the second stage. The first two stages were not difficult for me, in fact I was very excited about my new direction in life. A whole new dimension and way of seeing life had now opened up to me. Little did I realize that stage three was where my desire for spiritual liberation would be tested in a way that I could not have imagined. This is the stage that many are not currently able to fully enter because of their strong identification with the ego. I will expound on stage three and stage four in later chapters.

I also want to mention that many souls in the younger generation have come into the earth already much more aware of truth than most souls of the past generations. Many of these souls from the younger generation will not have to go through all four of the stages that I have referred to. This was made possible by the souls who have prepared the way before them. We are definitely in a new age.

We are currently in a time of the most miraculous transformation that this world has ever seen. The opportunities for spiritual transformation have never been so available to the masses. In this age many souls will be able to move into the 5th dimension without physically dying. In the 1960s, a singing group called the 'Impressions' recorded a song called, 'People get Ready' which was a song about a train that was picking up people from coast to coast, but a person had to be ready to get aboard. In the same way, we must do whatever we can to prepare ourselves to get aboard this spiritual train of transformation which is happening all over the world. This spiritual transformation will carry us into a higher dimension filled with much greater light, life and love. When Jeshua walked the earth, he stated that he had come to bring us a more abundant life. We now have the opportunity to partake of that abundant life, if we choose to let go of darkness and choose the spiritual light within us. Our true nature consists of such deep joy and love which earthly treasures could never come close to matching.

My search for truth was not an easy journey for me and yet there is nothing else and no other path that I would have preferred to travel. I have now reached a state of mind in which I can say unequivocally that there is no other path which can compare to the fulfillment one experiences on the spiritual journey. All the difficulties and pain dissolve into a deep sense of fulfillment that one experiences as his spiritual unfoldment takes place. Each soul must make this journey for himself, although he will receive plenty of help on the way. Others can light the way and make it easier to see the obstacles on the path, but actually walking this path is the task each soul must do on their own.

We will receive exactly what we need each step of the way. A neophyte on the spiritual path may not have the awareness to assimilate deeper spiritual concepts until they gain greater spiritual light. A neophyte on the spiritual journey has nothing to do with the amount of time he has been on the spiritual journey in this lifetime. A soul in this lifetime can be ten years old and have greater light that another soul who has been on the spiritual journey for 30 years. It is the light and wisdom of the soul over many lifetimes that I am referring to.

A new soul on the path will not be able to understand many of the deeper truths. Imagine a person living in a completely darkened house for years without any light whatsoever. Now what do you think would happen if that person had maintained his ability to see and were to walk out of his completely darkened house into a very bright sunny day? He would be blinded by the light as his eyes would not be able to take the brilliance of the light. Instead, he would slowly have to adjust his eyes to the light. A small candle could be lit a couple of rooms from where the man is. Gradually he would be able to walk into the room where the candle is lit without being uncomfortable. After a while a soft lamp could be lit and so on. Therefore in this book I have used a number of stories and analogies to portray ideas in a way which I hope will clarify the ideas I am relaying.

I know absolutely that this world is not real, that it exists only in our minds as a dream and yet I again want to stress that this dream is playing a very important role in the expansion of the creation of God. I know how real it seems to be because I have experienced my fair share of pain in this life and many others. As the light within one grows so does the compassion for the suffering that mankind is enduring. Learning to see with spiritual insight will eventually lead to the end of all suffering. This new way of seeing is through the eyes of perfect innocence, which will eventually open our spiritual sight and bring about the awakening from this dream.

If this world is not real, as you say, why does is seem so real to everyone?

I will explain this idea in many ways throughout this book. For now, let me tell you a story to hopefully shed some light on how this dream seemed to manifest.

Once there were two small boys who had the most loving parents imaginable. The father owned the fanciest restaurant in all the land. People would come from all parts of the world to eat at his restaurant because the food was so delicious. The selection of foods at the restaurant was unlimited whether it was for a child of three or a master gourmet chef. Another thing unique about this restaurant was that the food was all free.

The father had more money than he could ever spend so he saw no need to charge for the food. He just loved seeing the happy faces of the people after they had eaten a big meal. The mother was a most loving, nurturing and happy woman who loved her children more than anything. They lived in a beautiful mansion with servants who were ready to meet any needs the children had. The children had countless playmates and they played in the vast expanse on the grounds of the mansion. The children were literally in paradise.

One summer night as the younger son got ready for bed, something very strange happened. A very charming young man appeared to him out of nowhere and told the son that he could have his own restaurant which would be even better than his father's. People would come from all over to eat at his restaurant and he would become very famous. The younger son loved the idea of owning his own restaurant and being famous. He asked his visitor how he could do this. The charming man told him that he would take care of everything and to pack what he needed and leave his father's land. Without a word to his parents or brother he gathered many of his father's servants and left the grounds of the mansion in the middle of the night and went out on his own. He had great ambitions of building his own restaurant where he would charge people large sums of money to eat there, not like his father who gave it away. After many days of travel, the son finally reached the end of his father's grounds and entered into a very dry and desolate place. The son decided that this would be the place where he would build his restaurant so that he could intercept people going to his father's restaurant and have them eat at his place. His servants were told to build a restaurant and surrounding lodgings similar to his father's. When the restaurant was completed, the son told his servants to start enticing travelers into the restaurant by whatever means necessary.

The food at the son's restaurant tasted very bad in comparison to his father's and many people got very sick after eating at the son's restaurant but he added entertainment which distracted the customers. When people started complaining about the food, the son simply added more glitz to his entertainment to distract people from how they felt. He also charged exorbitant prices, but people paid the price because of the alluring entertainment. Meanwhile the son's parents would daily send their servants to bring the boy home, but the boy refused.

After a number of years a great drought hit the land where the son lived and there was no food to serve the customers. The son began to starve and so he began begging for food from people who were on the way to eat at his father's restaurant. They told the son that there was no need to go hungry because there was a restaurant on the grounds of the mansion where he could have all the food he wanted for free. The son got angry at the people when they told him this and yelled and cursed at them for telling him such a ridiculous lie. He had forgotten who he was.

The boy's parents were now very concerned because the boy would curse and beat the servants whom they had sent to bring him home, accusing them of lying to him and wanting to take his property, which by the way was absolutely worthless. Finally his parents decided to send the elder son to fetch his younger brother before he died of starvation. They thought that if their lost son would see his brother, that he might come to his senses and return home. When the elder brother saw his sibling, his heart almost broke. Here was his brother, heir to a vast fortune, in rags, emaciated and starving. He also saw that the light had gone out of his younger brother's eyes and he knew that it would be difficult to communicate with him. The older brother started telling his brother about their home and how it was filled with unlimited bounty, beauty, joy and love and that all he needed to do was to return home with him and he would be welcomed with the greatest and most joyful party he could imagine. For a moment there was even a little bit of recognition in the younger brother's eyes.

Now wouldn't you the reader think that there is really no decision for the lost brother to make here? It's a slam dunk. You go home with your brother to a land where the word 'lack' does not exist. But no, after hearing his brother, the lost son decided that his brother was also lying to him and started beating him with a stick and chased him away. When the parents heard of this they were very sad.

The beautiful mansion and restaurant are symbolic of our true home. The dry desolate place where the son built his own restaurant is symbolic of the physical world and a state of mind separated from God. The charming young man who appeared to the son is symbolic of the unbalanced ego.

Now let's end the story with a happy ending. Because of his suffering, hunger and loneliness, the younger son finally had a heart opening and realized his great mistake and began his long journey home. After a very long and arduously journey the son could finally see the mansion in the distance and his heart was filled with joy. Just then the alarm clock went off and the younger son woke up and realized he had been dreaming. It had been a dreadful dream and he was so happy that none of that had actually happened. He ran to his father's and mother's bedroom and gave them a big hug. He then went to his older brother's bedroom and gave him a big hug also. When the parents and brother of the younger son saw him, they recognized that there was something very different about the son. He seemed to be emanating more light and wisdom than the day before. They realized that something very dramatic had happened to him during the night.

This story contains a great truth. A Course in Miracles beautifully portrays this truth throughout the book. Understanding who we are and our purpose on earth, will be a great light and help us to awaken from this dream.

How do we start the process of waking up?

The process begins with a conscious decision on our part to discover what is real. A strong desire to know the truth is necessary to embark on our journey to awakening.

Why is that?

Imagine that you are lost in a deep dark cave and have no idea how to get out. Many have tried to get out of the cave but were never heard from again. More than anything you desire to find your way out of the cave. Finally one person discovers the way out and comes back with a map which shows you how to free yourself. You must follow the map precisely in order to find your way out otherwise you will continue to be trapped in the dark cave.

The map represents the truth. The truth is a great spiritual light which illumines our perception. Without light, we will continue to stumble around in the darkness of this world. The spiritual light coming into the world at this time is so powerful that it won't take as much effort to find our way out of the darkness. The Holy Spirit, that part of our mind which is connected to God, is our key in helping us to awaken from this nightmare we are dreaming. This part of our mind knows that the world is not real but also knows that we believe it is real. His job is to help us awaken to the knowing that we are innocent and that the seeming separation from God never actually occurred.

We don't have to try and become perfect to enter paradise. We only have to realize that we have never done anything wrong. Many people believe we have to be a spiritual martyr and continually offer sacrifices to God to get into heaven. God does not desire sacrifices. When we offer sacrifices to atone for our so called sins, we are giving reality to the sins for which we are offering sacrifices. God only wants us to awaken to the great reality of who we are. I will say something now that may shock many people. It is not what you physically do in the world that determines your awakening. Your actions have nothing to do with it. Your awakening will come when your mind is transformed and aligned with truth. The true transformation takes place in our mind.

Are you saying that I can do anything I want if my thoughts are in accord with truth?

Please don't think that what I am saying gives a person license to do whatever he wants. I have mentioned before and will continue to say that everything that seems to be happening outside of us is really happening in our mind. The images projected by our mind will always be in accord with our beliefs, whether we are consciously aware of the beliefs or not. A person cannot claim to be spiritually awake and continue to do things that are harmful to himself or others. Jeshua said that you will know a tree by the fruit it bears. A person on the spiritual path will not ignore the suffering of others. We should do what we are led to do in helping to alleviate the suffering in the world. The important thing is our state of mind while we are helping others. The proper state of mind is to see the perfection in all those we are helping and thus we are seeing ourselves as perfect. We must be careful not to see them as their physical condition, because then we would just be giving more life and credence to an illusion in our mind. We can serve our fellow man best by acknowledging their spiritual perfection. It is a challenging process to see beyond the physical appearance of things and to try to see the perfection in all things. Yet, it is extremely important to develop this spiritual perspective because how we see the world and others is what we are creating for ourselves. Whenever we help anybody in any way, we are **literally** helping ourselves.

God doesn't care how good we believe we have been, or how many prayers we have said. He loves us all the same regardless of how we believe we have lived our lives. There is no such thing as a God that judges or punishes us. We don't have to repent for anything because, believe it or not, we have never done anything wrong. This world that we live in is a dream. Will we be punished for having a nightmare? The only one who punishes us is ourselves. We need to be loving, gentle and forgiving of ourselves so that we can forgive others as well. As we begin to more fully understand who we are, we will begin to have glimpses of the nature of God because this is truly who we are.

You seem to be saying that part of our spiritual purpose is to rid ourselves of all sense of individuality. Who would we be if we were to lose all sense of ourselves as an individual?

It would be pointless to put ourselves through the process of completely relinquishing the ego and the personal individuality if this process resulted in us losing all awareness of who we are. If our long and difficult journey of conquering our ego meant that we would blend into the omnipresence of God and lose all sense of us ever having existed as an individual, I would say to avoid the spiritual path at all cost because it would mean the obliteration of us as conscious beings. Quite the contrary, when we awaken spiritually, we will always maintain the awareness of who we are, even in the ultimate merging into our oneness with God. Instead of our losing awareness of who we are, we become more and more aware of the omnipresent love, power and beauty that we truly are and always have been. The individuality that will be dissolved in this process consists of everything that causes us pain and feelings of isolation and separation. This is the false ego that I write about in the chapter on the ego.

Where did our bodies and this physical universe come from if not from God?

This world, our bodies and the physical universe are not real. We are spiritually asleep and are having what seems to be a very vivid dream. The path back to reality requires us to go through a process of awakening to who we truly are. We need to open up to our inner spiritual light so that we can wake up from the dream we are having. As our inner light becomes brighter and brighter and we reach the final stage of spiritual development we will realize that we are God on earth.

To get a better idea of the seeming conundrum I am speaking about, you might want to rent a couple of movies which are based on the findings of quantum physics. The titles are 'What the Bleep do we Know' and the second one which goes into even more depth is, 'What the Bleep, down the Rabbit Hole'. Both movies explain in scientific terms that what we perceive and experience in our daily lives is all happening in our mind. There really is no physical world. The second movie explains that science can only take us as far as the idea of consciousness. Quantum physics is uncertain as to what consciousness is and how it came into being. A Course in Miracles explains that consciousness seemingly came into being as the first step in the seeming separation from God.

Many famous people have had very clear realizations of the illusion of this world. Edgar Allan Poe stated, "All that we see or seem is but a dream within a dream." Carl Jung, a great influential thinker of the 20th century said, "Who looks outside, dreams. Who looks inside, awakens." All that we seem to be experiencing here on earth is but a dream. It is not real.

20

CHAPTER 3

The Ego

I spoke about the first two stages of awakening earlier and so I will continue with stage three. Stage three is a very, very difficult phase to go through. This is a stage which will test the will of the spiritual aspirant. During this stage, there is a process of literal dying to the person we believed we were. Stage three of bringing my ego into balance was a constant battle for many years. Take heart, we are all unique and your stage three can be a lot shorter, especially during this day and age.

The ego is a necessary part of our lessons and growth in this realm of duality. There is nothing wrong with having an ego, but in this book I am addressing those who are seeking to transcend the unbalanced, separated ego and commune with God. Each soul has their own free will and may choose to keep the ego as long as they desire. There is absolutely no judgment as to how a soul chooses to live their lives. The question that each one must answer is whether we want to continue experiencing pain and separation, or divine love and peace.

I came face to face with my ego in a very intense way in my first year in the Holy Order of MANS. This definitely was the most difficult year I had yet experienced because of the constant battle between my ego and my will. The ego knew that its' very existence and seeming reality were being challenged because of the new path I had just entered. I experienced such intense discomfort mentally, emotionally and physically because of this conflict. Just about every day during that first year, I mentally had my bags packed and was out the door of the Order house and back into my old life. The only thing that prevented me from leaving was my overwhelming desire to fulfill whatever God's Will was for me here on earth. I also came to the realization that God's Will and mine are exactly the same and it is that will which motivates me on a daily basis. The ego did everything it could to persuade me to leave, but through the grace of God I was able to hang in there and let go of many layers of false beliefs, desires and fears which had been tormenting me for many years.

I was only in the Order for a little over four months when I received word that I would be going out on missionary work. This was highly unusual, because I had not even begun missionary classes. Usually a student would have to go to classes for some time before they were even considered for this work. There were many brothers and sisters who have been taking these classes much longer than I had even been in the Order. At that time there was a need for someone to go to Lincoln, Nebraska. Father Paul, the head of the Order, asked one of the teachers to go to the chapel to ask for guidance in choosing the right person to go on this mission. The teacher received, from spirit, that I was the one to go.

Now four days before I got word of this transfer, I woke up with the most massive headache I could imagine. For three days I laid in bed, unable to get up. I intuitively knew that there were some deep mental patterns in me which were being worked on. On the fourth day I was finally able to get out of bed. On that day I was called into Father Paul's office and he told me I would be leaving for Nebraska the very next day.

I left for Lincoln by bus on January 7, 1970. I had never been to the midwest and had no idea how cold it got there. I left so quickly that I didn't have the chance to gather any warm clothes or even an overcoat. There was one other brother there at the time and he picked me up at the bus station in an old noisy pick-up truck. We drove to the old house where we would be living which had no insulation whatsoever. There were only a couple of heating vents in the whole house which put out about as much heat as a few lit matches. It was freezing in the morning when we got up and the two of us would run and stand under one of the vents as we got dressed. This was all we could afford and this was to be our house during my time in Lincoln.

I got a job at a veterinary hospital cleaning out animal cages and assisting the doctor as she performed procedures on animals. The Order was totally self-sufficient and was supported by brothers and sisters holding outside jobs and turning over our paychecks to support the running of the Order.

The other brother and I would go on street mission every night except for weekends. We would leave the house about seven in the evening and walk the streets for two or three hours. The purpose was to make ourselves available to anyone who needed help. Needless to say we were the only ones walking the streets, at that time, during those extremely cold winter nights. The temperatures got close to zero and even lower on some nights. All I had on was a tee shirt, my cleric collar and a light dark jacket. After an hour or so we would go into a coffee shop to take a break. My mouth was so frozen that I had a hard time asking for coffee. When I look back at it now, it seems quite hilarious.

The nine months I spent in Lincoln were extremely difficult for me because of the constant and continuing daily battle between the ego and my will. In early spring of 1970, I was going through an especially dark period and felt that everything I was doing was useless. The thought of leaving the Order passed through my mind on a daily basis. On this particular day, I was experiencing a lot of mental and emotional darkness and felt that I was getting nowhere in my spiritual quest. I was sitting on the steps of our mission house in a very dark state when a very clear audible voice said to me, "Do not use reason to judge your spiritual growth." Even though the voice did not make me feel any better, at least it assured me that the way I was feeling was not an indication that I was not progressing on the path. In most cases, the darkest hours on our spiritual journey, become some of the most important steps in the alchemical process of our spiritual metamorphosis. Throughout my stay in the Order I received many beautiful spiritual nuggets from Jeshua. Towards the end of my stay in Nebraska Jeshua came to me and said, **"Persist ye in your striving and all channels of knowledge and service will be opened unto you."** These words were like a healing salve for all the inner turmoil I had been going through in my first year in the Order.

I will relate another experience I had during my second year in the Holy Order of MANS which will give you some idea of the hold the ego still had on me. I had returned from Nebraska and was back in San Francisco when this happened. In the Order we were all assigned daily chores in addition to our regular jobs, studies, classes, and spiritual work. At the time of this experience I was the head of the kitchen detail which was responsible for cleaning up the kitchen after meals. After we were all done washing the dishes, scrubbing the floors and general clean-up, I was to inspect the area to make sure everything was properly completed. The head cook would then come down afterwards to make sure we had done it properly. For whatever reason, the head cook and I just did not get along. You know the type of person that just rubs you the wrong way. We had already had a few disagreements in the short time we had known each other. After the clean-up, I was in my room studying when I heard someone on the intercom system calling my name and telling me that the head cook wanted to see me downstairs in the kitchen. I immediately knew that he was going to tell me the job had not been completed to his satisfaction. My ego immediately responded with a thought, "Who the hell does he think he is. We did the job exactly as it should have been done." I caught myself and told myself to calm down, to go listen to what he had to say and do whatever he said needed to be done, without any reaction. I knelt down for a moment and prayed for the peace to accept what the cook had to say without reacting. I walked down the stairs reminding myself to keep calm, to see him as my brother and accept what he had to say. I reached the bottom of the stairs and saw the cook standing at the end of the long hallway leading to the kitchen. As I walked towards him I kept praying for the peace to remain calm and not to react. When I reached him, he told me that the kitchen floor was still dirty. With immediate anger I responded,

"What do you mean the floor is dirty, I checked it and it is fine. You don't know what you are talking about. I'm not about to clean it again when it has already been done right." I was livid and of course I acted completely opposite to the way I intended. The ego still had my number and I knew it. This gives you a slight indication of the mountain I had to climb to reach a state of mind which would allow me to relinquish the ego. I know that my prayers for calm were heard, but there was still a ton of old beliefs and anger in me that needed to be released before I could experience the manifestation of the peace I so longed for.

The ego in itself is not bad. It is when we give it the power to control our lives that it becomes a little dictator. We will never lose our pure ego which is the uniqueness of who each one of us is. The ego allows each one of us to manifest in physical matter. If we did not have an ego, we would not be able to individualize. An analogy which might give you a clearer picture of the ego is to imagine the sun which shines upon the earth. The light of the sun is not individualized but simply shines all over. Now if we took a magnifying glass and allowed the light of the sun to shine through the glass, we are able to focus the sun light. We are in a sense individualizing part of it. In the same way, our true consciousness is infinite. Through the ego, we are able to individualize it in order to experience life here on earth.

Continuing with this analogy, the light of the sun can be focused to burn down a house, or to start a fire which will give warmth on a cold night. This is determined by our individual will and how we choose to focus it. An unbalanced ego will burn the house down, whereas a balanced ego will spread warmth and love wherever she goes. Our purpose on the spiritual path is to bring the ego into balance so that it can be used for the good of mankind.

The unbalanced ego can be likened to a guest who we invite into our house. This guest immediately begins to start wrecking the furniture and making a mess everywhere he goes in the house. He then starts insulting you every time he sees you and begins stealing your valuables. He also insults any of your friends who come over. You now realize how dangerous he is and begin to fear him. You become afraid that if you ask him to leave, he will harm you. He becomes so entrenched in your whole life that you forget how nice your life was before you invited him into your life. You learn to live in fear, not knowing what he is going to do next

How many of us would put up with a guest in our house who is threatening and criticizing us and our friends? A person would have to be a masochist to invite such a guest into their house even for a few minutes. What if I were to tell you that each one of us, except for the spiritually awake, has a visitor living with us 24 hours a day, who is even worse than the unwanted guest? At least the so called guest would be obvious in his negative actions and demeanor. Our internal guest is so subtle and cunning, that it is almost impossible to detect its presence. In fact this visitor is so devious that it makes us believe that we are who it is. It causes us to believe that we want exactly what it desires, even though it is the exact opposite of what we **truly** want. From the moment of its seeming inception, the unbalanced ego has been leading us down a path of pain and destruction.

Where is this illusive entity, called the ego, located? The ego is a state of mind, a mental identification with a false belief system. If we believe in lack and limitation, we are being controlled by the mind of the ego. The belief that we could actually separate ourselves from God seemed to have brought the false ego into existence. The ego lives in the belief that we are separate from each other. If we believe in judgment, we are supporting one of the pillars of the ego. Our belief in death perpetuates the ego. Some of the most powerful tools of deception that the ego has at its disposal are sin, guilt, and fear. We can list any negative or limited belief or attitude and we are looking directly at one of the mental pillars of the ego. When we honestly look at these beliefs in ourselves, we can see how deeply ingrained some of these concepts are. The majority of people on earth are totally identified with these beliefs. We assume that negativity and limitations are a natural part of life and don't even question their authenticity. That is why the ego has had its way in this world for so long.

Now that I have pointed out many of the flaws of the unbalanced ego, I again want to state that taking on the false ego and journeying into darkness is one of the greatest gifts that a soul can offer to God. I will expound on this idea in a later chapter.

Most of our religions have doctrines that say we are limited sinful creatures and we should repent for our sins. Unfortunately some religious institutions are fortresses of the ego and have done more harm than good when it comes to revealing truth. Jeshua spoke of the Scribes and the Pharisees and how they held the keys to the kingdom but would block people from entering in and would not enter in themselves. Many religious organizations don't even know the truth. If the religions of the world taught the truth, there would be no need for religious institutions because we would realize that the holy tabernacle and altar is within each of our hearts. The true worship takes place in the privacy of our minds and heart. Being raised a Catholic I know firsthand the damage to the soul that the confessionals do. In the confessional there is a reconfirmation that we are sinners and so Catholics and many others from different religions who preach sin and guilt are trapped in that belief system throughout their lives. In biblical times there was a belief that the sacrifice of animals would take away sins which is even more insane.

Even so, some of these religions perform a service for certain individuals because the more profound teachings would be very hard to understand by young souls. Jeshua told his disciples that he had many more things to tell them, but at that time they were unable to hear or understand what he had to say. So he spoke to them on the level they were able to comprehend. We are in a time where many people across the world are now able to hear and understand the truth that will set them free.

The ego will try and do everything in its power to keep us asleep. To know the truth is the last thing the ego wants for us, because truth is the light that brings about the obliteration of the unbalanced ego. The ego seemed to come into being out of darkness and cannot endure the light of truth. The only thing that gives the ego life is our belief that it is real. Once we start opening up to the light all our false beliefs begin to disappear. When the ego finally dissolves into the nothingness from whence it came, we are reborn into the light and into our union with God.

What if some of our beliefs are really true, why should we let go of them?

Let me assure you that anything that is true will remain after a person goes through the transformation. It is impossible for truth to be destroyed. I know this seems like a big price to pay, but we must understand that it is our false beliefs and identifications that have created all our fears, pains and unhappiness. In reality what we are giving up is **nothing** in exchange for **everything**. If a person really understood the magnitude of that last statement he would immediately begin to search for the truth that will set him free. There would be no price too big to pay. Jeshua put it in another way when he said, "He who would give up his life, will find life." The life Jeshua is asking us to give up is the false, limited, and painful life that the ego has seemingly created. Why would we not want to give up that which conceals our true nature of love and joy?

Most spiritual students have heard of the 'Dark night of the Soul'. My journey through this third stage of letting go of my false ego, consisted of many of these dark periods. All the concepts of who I thought I was and which I had reinforced over many years of habitual reactions were totally challenged by the light of truth which started to penetrate my belief system in 1969. These challenges were vehemently resisted by the ego. The conflict that was going on between the ego and the light created some very intense discomfort in my physical, emotional and mental bodies. Had it not been for my total desire to fulfill God's Will, there is no way I would have continued on the path that I was travelling. It doesn't mean I would have given up my spiritual journey, it just means I would have tried to find an easier path back to God. Eventually though, if I were seeking true liberation, I would have had to face and unravel my ego regardless of what path I chose. We must face our own darkness in order to move into the light. The greater the darkness that we face, the greater the light will be when we wake up.

Alright, so how do we give up the unbalanced ego that we believe we are?

First of all we must have a desire to know the truth more than anything else. If we don't have this overwhelming desire to know who we really are, we are defeated before we begin the journey. My desire to fulfill God's Will was the engine that propelled me on my journey. Our desire to know the truth above all else will allow us to honestly assess our current situation without judgment or condemnation. We have to look into all the corners and dark recesses of our mind to understand what has been driving us. In order to see more clearly we need more spiritual light. The process of letting go of our false beliefs and receiving more light happens simultaneously. For example, if we detect that we have a lot of resentment against someone, we must then make a sincere effort to understand that any resentment we have is really against our own self, because everything we experience is happening in our own mind. It is our dream and our dream only. Eventually we will realize that resentment, or any other negative or limited idea, comes from a false belief of who we are. The foundation of this false belief is based on the belief that we are separate from God and from others. I cannot overestimate the importance of this understanding.

All we need is a little willingness which will lead to greater willingness which will eventually lead us to the final step of awakening from this dream of illusion. The great benefit of taking our first small step is that we will receive as much help in this process as we can accept. Remember this whole process is taking place in our mind. We then need to live and think the truth as much as possible. The transformation process will bring about a new perception of our self and others. Our physical and material conditions may not necessarily change that much, but our outlook and attitude will be totally transformed.

Let me give you an analogy of what is taking place in this process. Imagine that you are in a large cluttered room that is completely dark and you keep bumping into the debris that fills the room and continually hurt yourself. You are aware that you have to clean up this room if you want to stop hurting yourself. You cannot see because of the darkness, but you can feel all the junk in the room because you keep stumbling into it wherever you turn. You have no idea where you can put all the clutter, but you decide you have to begin somewhere. You decide to start moving it to one side of the room to see if there is a door or window which will allow some light into the room so that you can see. You move a few pieces of junk to one side and to your amazement and joy you see a tiny shaft of light coming from the area in which you have been clearing. Having seen this first glimmer of light gives you hope and inspiration to clean up more of the clutter. As you clear more of the junk, more light fills the room until you catch a glimpse of a doorway which had been covered up by all the clutter. You now realize that the door had always been open and you see a world outside which is more beautiful than you could have ever imagined. This gives you even more enthusiasm to work even harder to totally clear the path to the doorway. As even more light comes into the room, you notice that there have been others in the room helping you to move all this clutter, even though you had not seen them until now. They were anxiously waiting for you to take the first step so that they could assist you in the clearing process. Finally, with the assistance of your invisible helpers, the path to the doorway is completely clear and you walk out into the sunlight into a world of infinite beauty and joy.

The junk in the room represents our false beliefs, identifications and desires of the ego. Moving the junk in the dark represents the beginning of our willingness to let go of some of our false beliefs. The light beaming into the room represents our own inner light which naturally shines as we are willing to truthfully face ourselves and begin letting go of our limited and destructive beliefs. The invisible helpers are spiritual guides and angels who want to assist us in finding truth. The door into the outside world represents a state of spiritual awakening which a person experiences as he begins dissolving his false identity. This spiritual awakening leads to an inner experience of complete peace and contentment.

Do not think you have to let go of all illusions immediately to be successful. It is a matter of taking the first little step. No step is too small. The foundation for this change must be based on the desire to know who we truly are. Truth is available in many forms to anyone who is sincerely seeking.

The process of awakening includes letting go of all our beliefs in right or wrong, good or evil. We need to understand that it is just as important not to identify with the good that happens through us, because this is as big a trap as identifying with the harmful actions. The reason for this is that as long as we identify with either good or evil, we are comparing it to the other and we thus remain stuck in duality. The journey into Christ Consciousness necessitates that we recognize that darkness is the other half of light. Our focus must be on that which underlies both. We must be the awareness which observes all that is taking place, without judgment or identification with either. This does not mean that we sanction evil or that we do not make an effort to help others out of the darkness, if that is what they choose. We simply do not judge the darkness as we lead others to the light.

As we take on more light, we will be filled with compassion as we observe the darkness which others are subjected to, but we do not judge those who are committing the offenses. We recognize that the law of cause and effect is perfectly bringing everything into balance. The light that we carry as enlightened beings is a strong beacon to all whom are open to receiving it. Each person is their own creator and must make the decision as to when they choose to follow the light. We can be a great light in the world, but we cannot force others to follow the light. This is because of the gift of free will that our Creator has bestowed upon each one of us. A soul can choose to remain asleep as long as they desire with no judgment from God, but they will have to experience the effects of their actions as long as they are caught up in duality.

It is impossible to see the truth if we don't first dissolve some of our false beliefs which block the light of truth from reaching our awareness. Jeshua said, "Seek and you shall find." Our seeking for truth is the beginning of this effort. There will come a time in a person's spiritual development when he or she will even have to give up seeking. I will expound on this idea more fully in a later chapter.

The ego comes in all forms, shapes, and appearances and can appear as timid, angry, sad, happy, loving, and confident. Now being happy, loving, and confident may seem like attractive traits, but if these attributes are supported by the ego, it is only a fragile façade as there is no real joy behind these facades. There is actually a great deal of fear behind these false facades. The exterior facade of love and joy that the ego projects can be overshadowed at any moment by the fear that lurks underneath.

I grew up with a very big chip on my shoulder because of the loss of my mom and the feeling of being rejected by my dad. The harsh treatment I was subjected to in the orphanage also played a big role in creating a very insecure and angry personality. After my dad took me out of the orphanage at age ten, I became a person who was ready to fight at the drop of a hat. I got in many fights throughout high school because of all the pent up anger due to my childhood experiences. Because of all my insecurities, it was very, very difficult for me not to react to others if I perceived even the slightest judgment or offense against me.

There was a time in my early twenties when I was so afraid of my own ego, because of the control it had over me, that I had to think twice before going to parties because I was concerned that if somebody did or said something I did not like, my ego would cause me to get in a fight. I did not like to fight, but because of the big insecure ego I had at the time, I was not really in control. The ego was ruling a big part of my personality and my life at that time.

The ego has most of us just where it wants us. The ego holds its greatest power over us in its ability to convince us that we are guilty for some imagined sin and therefore must fear God because He will punish us. We may not be consciously aware of the guilt, but if we are still caught up in fear of any kind, then we can be sure that underneath the fear is a feeling of guilt. As long as fear, desire and guilt are part of our belief system we are still caught up in the ego's grip.

Fear is a big part of a person's life when the ego is in control. The reason for this is that if we are not spiritually awake we are living in darkness and one of the principle attributes of darkness is fear, regardless of how well it is hidden from others or from ourselves. In this world the ego is synonymous with a person's identity. The ego has lived its whole life through us, yet most people don't have the faintest idea that this ego wants nothing more than to destroy us.

Why would the ego want to destroy us if it has gone through the trouble of having us believe in it?

Because deep down the ego is aware that in reality it has no existence. It also knows that our true nature is eternal and it feels that if it can destroy us, maybe it can steal our eternal nature. The ego is extremely cunning and at the same time totally insane.

I mentioned earlier that the belief in death is one of the most powerful tools the ego has to keep us chained to the illusion of this world. I know it is difficult not to believe in death when death seems to be a natural part of our earthly cycle. One thing that needs to be understood is that we are not the body and cannot possibly die. I'm not saying that you have to overcome the death of the body to become spiritually awake. I am saying that the realization that death is an illusion becomes a natural part of our knowing as we awaken spiritually. The only death we must experience to be free, is the death of the ego. When a person has completed the relinquishment of his ego, his physical death will be no more of a trauma than walking from one room into another room of extreme beauty and joy.

The ego will not give up control easily as it has the same self-preservation instinct that any living entity has. It is very aware when a person starts his journey on the spiritual path and this is when it becomes most ferocious and cunning. I remember an experience I had many years ago which will shed some light on this subject. It was during a period when a lot of my emotional baggage from childhood was surfacing. I was at home sitting on the sofa experiencing a lot of mental insecurities dealing with childhood issues of abandonment and unworthiness. In years past a mental barrage like this would have sent me into a depressed state, but I just sat there watching my thoughts with no attachment or judgment as to what was taking place in my mind. All of a sudden my consciousness seemed to be transported to the center of my being where I continued watching my mental process, only now it seemed as if I were in a protective bubble where none of the heavy feelings associated with these thoughts could affect me. From this vantage point I could see very clearly the ego operating through these dark thoughts. As the ego became aware that I was watching and

33

was not being affected by the thoughts, it changed its strategy and started flattering me and telling me how good I was and how I should be proud of myself. Of course I didn't buy into that either, but it was a great insight into how cunning and illusive the ego can be, because when it can't get you one way, it will try another.

The ego is a master when it comes to deception and it knows all our weaknesses. It doesn't care whether we are suffering, poor or rich. The ego knows that any of these experiences will most likely keep us asleep and eventually cause us pain, which is the objective of the ego. You might wonder why your own ego would want to cause you misery. The ego maintains its existence through deceiving us into identifying with the joy, success, pain and misery that seems to be happening in our life. It wants us to keep believing in this world of illusion because if we stopped believing, the ego would die. Failure and success are two of the life paths that the ego uses to keep us from discovering our true identity. It is afraid that once we begin questioning things, we will begin to recognize that we are something much more than the ego. This questioning and contemplation of the meaning of life will eventually lead to truth and the dissolution of the ego. So the ego wants to keep us very busy, either in our misery or in striving to accomplish something special which promises great rewards. Sometimes the attainment of worldly rewards does seem to bring temporary satisfaction, but in time it will never satisfy and will always keep a person striving to get even more.

Who am I? Where am I going? What is life all about? Is this all there is? These are the types of questions that come from your true Self. The ego wants no part of these questions. It wants to keep us in the dark which is the only place it can seemingly exist and continue its deception. The ego must be taken out of the darkness and placed in the light of our consciousness in order to understand its false nature.

Do you have any suggestions as to how I might become more aware of my ego? How can I become more aware of my moment by moment thought process?

A mountain climber, who is making a very difficult climb, must be totally aware of his every movement. To lose concentration even for a moment could be fatal. In the same way, if we would practice giving our full attention to what we are doing each moment, we would begin to take control of our thought process, which is a huge step in our awakening. The concentration exercises I describe at the end of this book can be of great assistance in helping you to control your mind. The ego does not like it when we are critiquing our thoughts, because believe it or not, most of the thoughts going through our mind are not our own. Unless a person is spiritually awake, the thoughts he is having are being thought by the ego. The ego is the writer of the life script for the majority of people in this world. Most people cannot quiet their minds, even for a few seconds. They do not realize that all the thoughts running through their minds are responsible for their so called reality. To take control of our lives, we must take control of our thoughts.

Get in the habit of constantly observing your thoughts, without any judgment or interpretation. The practice of observing our thoughts is a very powerful way to start understanding the ego. Being aware of the thoughts that are passing through our mind, will give us the power to start choosing which thoughts we choose to give power to and which thoughts we choose to negate.

Spiritual students have been using the practice of 'impersonal self-observation' for a long time. There is a good book I read many years ago which really gave me a lot of insight into this practice. It is entitled: **'The Mystic Path to Cosmic Power'** by Vernon Howard. In the book Vernon Howard refers to the ego as the 'false self' of which there are many faces. There are many great books out now that shed light on the subject of the ego. Eckhart Tolle's book, 'The Power of Now' gives the reader great insight into the ego/pain body.

Jeshuas' life was the antithesis of the ego. Jeshua took on the mission to display in this third dimension the process a person must go through in order to fully awaken spiritually. This does not mean we have to go through the literal crucifixion, but it does mean we must go through the difficult process of giving up our ego. The crucifixion was a living symbolic expression of the voluntary relinquishment of the ego. It is represented in the words, "Not my will, but Yours be done." Jeshua sacrificed his life so that greater spiritual light could enter the world so that his brothers and sisters on earth could begin to see the truth. He lived his life as a way of creating a path to spiritual transformation which was represented by his resurrection.

Each of us will have to go through this process of relinquishing the ego in our own way. Remember, that each person who awakens makes it that much easier for all those who are following on the path to liberation.

Why is that?

We are all part of one mind. When a part of the mind becomes enlightened, it sheds light on the entire mind, which makes it easier for other parts of that same mind to awaken.

There are cases when an individual experiences a sudden awakening through no seeming spiritual effort of their own in this lifetime. Individuals like this have most likely done a lot of spiritual work in the past and are ripe for the awakening when the time presents itself. Spiritual awakenings come in different degrees depending of the development of the soul having the awakening. A person who fully awakens to his oneness with God and lives in that state all the time will most likely have full access to all knowledge. He would have the power to heal the sick and in some cases even raise the dead. A fully awakened person would not perform an act like that just to prove his spiritual power to others. He does only what he is guided to do by the Holy Spirit. He doesn't care what others think of him. His only concern is to help his brothers and sisters who are sincere in their desire to awaken.

Many may find it difficult to accept that this world is a dream, an illusion, because everything seems so real and substantial. Let's look at this idea in a way we can all relate to. Have you ever had a dream which was so vivid that you were sure it was actually taking place, only to wake up in the morning to realize it was a dream? I remember when I was about 11 years old, I had a series of dreams that continued from one night to the next like a television serial and it seemed so real. One night the dream ended at a very interesting point and I could not wait to get to bed the next night to see what was going to happen. I have also had vivid dreams in which I had gotten into trouble with the law and it seemed so real that when I woke up I was so relieved that I felt like celebrating. It was as if I had actually been given a reprieve from a jail sentence or something even worse.

Yes, but the reason we couldn't distinguish a dream from reality is that we were asleep, we were not conscious.

This is just my point, the majority of the world is asleep and not aware that they are participating in a vivid dream here on earth. There is absolutely no judgment in this statement. We have all been asleep and we will all awaken. The spiritual path is for those who have had enough of the insanity and are ready to wake up. It is extremely important not to judge another who chooses to take the path of the ego and experience the darker side of life. This may be exactly what the soul needs at this time.

Imagine that you had a favorite sister who had gotten so involved in a television program that when one of the characters on the program died, your sister went into a deep depression. She could not eat or sleep and would not leave the house. Wouldn't you try everything you could think of to wake her out of her misery? You would probably want to shake her and get it into her head that the program is not real and that the characters are only acting. I know this sounds a little farfetched, but as a person begins the awakening process he will begin to see right through the illusion which had held him prisoner for many lifetimes. The only reason we cannot awaken from this dream is because of the guilt, fears and beliefs we hold unto. It is the light of truth that can set us free from this illusion. All true spiritual teachers have come into the world to bear witness to the truth by allowing the light within them to shine so brightly that it allows those around them to begin to see the truth.

Why do you keep repeating the idea that this world is not real, that it is all a bad dream?

Repetition is absolutely necessary in the process of awakening. We all have lived many dream cycles, which many refer to as reincarnations. During all these many cycles we have reinforced our belief in the illusion over and over again. From the day we were born into our current cycle, we have been bombarded 24 hours a day with the idea that the world we live in is real. The reason I keep repeating the idea that this world is an illusion, is because it is necessary to reinforce this idea so that it can start breaking down all these false concepts and beliefs, which are the foundation of the world and the ego.

The way of escape from the ego's world of illusion into reality has been taught by many great teachers of the past. Siddhartha Gautama, who became known as the Buddha after his spiritual awakening, stated that this world is impermanent and that whatever is impermanent is by its very nature illusory and not of God. All things created by God are perfect and eternal. Buddha encouraged his followers to become aware of illusion through correct understanding. The words of these awakened beings are now being understood and practiced by many people in this day and age. Many people around the world are now starting to wake up from this very vivid dream that we have been having.

I want to give you a question to ponder regarding the ego. **Where does the darkness go when the light is turned on?** That's exactly where the ego goes when a person fully wakes up spiritually.

Before I conclude this chapter on the ego, I want to clarify one thing. The ego that I have referred to in this chapter is a fabrication of our false beliefs and has no reality outside the world of illusion. But there is another Ego, one that transcends all limitation and which knows itself to be glory beyond measure. This is the Ego that comes with the awareness that we are one with God, made in Her image with infinite power, joy, peace and love. This pure Ego knows that it is holy and perfect in every way and could not be otherwise. The difference between this Ego and the illusionary ego is that the pure Ego does not compare itself with anything or anyone else. It is aware of the holy oneness of all things. The unbalanced ego is something we created and have embraced through our ignorance. We become more and more aware of our pure Ego as we progress on our spiritual journey. We will always have an Ego, but it will be an omnipresent Ego. God has created us in His own image as an extension of Her Self to enjoy and expand the glory of His unlimited, ever expanding creation. This is the amazing truth of who we truly are.

My Fear of Intimacy

The death of my mom and loss of my family when I was four years old was very traumatizing and it had a very strong impact on how I interacted with women for a great portion of my life. I **unconsciously** sought out relationships which could not work out, or in which the woman was already committed. It wasn't until years later that I found out why I was choosing women who were already taken. It was a way of protecting myself from being abandoned. If the woman was already taken, then I could not be abandoned because she was not available. It was a safe relationship. In other relationships, I found ways to sabotage the relationship so it wouldn't work out. This unconscious way of dealing with women did not really work to protect me from pain as I still felt much devastation in the loss of these women. Note – other than my late partner, Linda, I have changed the names of the women I will be referring to in this chapter.

Because of my insecurity, real love was something that eluded me for a good portion of my life. I had girlfriends through whom I was hoping to fill the emptiness within. I thought I knew what the word 'love' meant, but what I was really seeking in my relationships was someone to fill the huge void I was feeling inside. Yet, when I had the chance to intimately open up to one of my partners, I ran for the hills.

I remember when I was a junior in high school, I had a big crush on a really cute girl who I would often see walking around school. I dreamed of going out with her. My heart would beat faster every time I saw her walk by. Her name was JoAnn and she was everything I could ever want in a girl. Finally one day I walked up to her and asked her to the Christmas dance. She told me she was going steady. I told her that I would talk to her boyfriend. She was surprised that I said that and replied that she would talk to him and work it out. I later found out that they had broken up because of her choosing to go to the dance with me. Our time together at the Christmas dance was amazing, it was the perfect date. There was such a connection between us and the evening seemed like a dream come true. When the night ended, we said goodnight with the understanding that we would be seeing much, much more of each other.

The next morning when I woke up and was asked about my date, I did not even want to hear her name. I didn't want anything to do with her. I never talked to her again. She kept asking one of my sisters about me but I just couldn't open up to the idea of being with her. I couldn't understand why I was acting that way, all I knew was there was a part of me that couldn't be with her. It wasn't until many years later that I came to the understanding that my strong feelings for JoAnn were a real threat to my safety. I had lost the most important woman in my life in childhood, my mother, and because of that I was put in an institution in which I was beaten and not allowed to express who I was. Unconsciously I feared that it was dangerous to be with someone like JoAnn because of the fear of loss. My unconscious fear was superimposed on JoAnn. On the conscious level, I really wanted to be with JoAnn and so my sub-conscious mind took over to protect me from the possible loss of her. Throughout my life, this unconscious fear played a big part in my relationships with women.

Love is the most powerful force in creation. In fact it is the power and motivating force that created all things. In A Course in Miracles, Jeshua states that Divine Love is beyond anything that can be taught. It is a state of being which manifests when a soul has surrendered all sense of being separate from God and others. Spiritual truths serve as a guide to help us let go of everything that blocks the experience of our true nature. Although pure love is not something that can be taught, a person can have an experience of this ecstatic state and know beyond any shadow of a doubt that unconditional love is who she is.

In this world, the term love comes in many forms. There is romantic love, familial love, love of country, etc. The love of a mother for her child is one of the most powerful types of personal love. Another type of love is the love a husband has for his wife, or the wife for her husband. Love that is founded on deep respect and consideration for the other is a very beautiful and powerful type of love. We all seek love because we hope that through the other person we can find that pure unconditional love that dwells within our own heart. Each soul has a deep desire to return to that state of unconditional love with God but most souls on earth are not consciously aware of it. Since we have forgotten the truth, we seek so many outlets to try and fill the void we feel inside. This world cries out for love but since we don't know where to find it, our cries manifest in so many painful and disappointing ways.

In A Course in Miracles, it is stated that the negative actions of people in the world are a cry out for love. Just as a baby cries out for her mother or for food, our seemingly hateful acts represent a crying out in pain for that love that we intuitively know is our true divine nature. If we would practice seeing the acts of hatred and violence of others as a crying out for love, instead of judging the act itself, we would take a huge step towards the state of divine wisdom.

In this world, the most common way people seek love is through the search for a mate. Most relationships provide a temporary haven, but unless the two individuals are spiritually mature, the relationship usually doesn't allow for much spiritual growth and instead creates a lot of pain, confusion and frustration. Relationships also present us the opportunity to see ourselves very clearly, as if looking in a mirror, so that we can see what traits in ourselves we need to release. It takes a spiritually mature soul to use conflicts in a relationship as a way of understanding themselves better.

One of my assignments in the Holy Order of Mans was to run a Community Center in Portland, Oregon. A Community Center is a group of lay people who wanted to follow the teachings of the Order, but for one reason or another could not take vows and enter the Order itself. My responsibilities there were to serve the sacraments, teach classes and give counsel to members when they sought it. In the morning I would serve communion to members before they went to work. One of the women in the community would set up the altar each morning and straighten up after the service. Her name was Marie, a beautiful soul who was married with one child. After everyone left and I finished my morning meditation, Marie and I would sit around and talk. We were totally comfortable with each other and had a lot of fun just talking.

One morning, several months later, Marie asked if she could join me in my post communion meditation in my room. I naively saw nothing wrong with her meditating with me so I agreed. The next morning after the communion services, she joined me in my room for meditation. We were in meditation about 20 minutes when I felt her lean over and kiss me. This took me by surprise and my first impulse was to immediately offer a prayer for strength and guidance so that this act would have no further consequence. For the next month or so, I tried to avoid having time alone with her, but soon we were back in the routine of having breakfast together and talking. We started doing other things together during the day, such as taking walks or going out for coffee. Deep inside I knew this was a big mistake, but my desires were now in the driver's seat. As time passed we became bolder and less discrete in our encounters and pretty soon there was talk in the community of our inappropriate relationship.

Eventually word got back to the Order headquarters and I was called back and made to appear before the Order Council to answer for what I had done. Before any decision was made by the Council, I was ordered to spend 40 days and nights in the chapel in complete silence, coming out only to use the bathroom, wash up and eat. The first few days in the chapel were very difficult, as my desire for Marie was still very strong and I seriously contemplated leaving the Order and going back to Portland to see if Marie and I could make a go of it. My desire to fulfill God's Will for me on earth was even stronger and so I remained. Towards the end of my stay in the chapel, I started having beautiful spiritual experiences. The time in the chapel on silence brought me to a state in which I connected with God in such a powerful way that I was talking to God, as if She were present right next to me. About three years after this experience in the chapel is when Jeshua appeared to me in a dream and told me he was going to place me on a different path. A month later I left the Order for good.

Three years after leaving the Order, I met a woman who I was with for the next 29 years. As you might guess, she was also married at the time of our meeting. Her name was Linda, but I called her "Little" which was a nickname I had for her from the very beginning of our relationship. I met Little in July of 1981. I had moved to Marin County in California a couple of years before meeting her. Our meeting took place at a spiritual lecture given by a swami on the Guru/Disciple relationship in San Anselmo, California. Little told me later that she recognized me the moment I walked through the door into the lecture hall. After the lecture she approached me and we began talking as if we had known each other all our lives. She radiated light and a love for life which immediately attracted me to her.

At that time, Little was hosting a weekly meditation program at her house once a week. She invited me to come to one of the meditation meetings, which I did. It was at that time that I found out that she was married. I continued going to the weekly meditation gatherings at her house every week and because her husband worked on Friday evenings, Little and I would go to the ashram together every Friday evening. Very quickly our relationship began to take on a greater intensity as the attraction to each other was very obvious. I suffered physically, emotionally and mentally because of my involvement with another married woman. My stomach started burning so bad that I had to carry a bottle of Mylanta with me at work to ease the pain. This burning went on for over a year. A religious person would say that God was punishing me for my actions, but this is obviously not the case. Our purpose of entering this world of duality is to experience both good and bad, the light and dark aspects of this illusion. I was suffering because I was judging myself in the sense that I intuitively knew that my actions were not in accord with the Light that I was seeking. It was my own personal guilt and self-condemnation which was causing my pain.

Eventually Little and her husband divorced and a couple of years later I moved in with her. The beginning of this new phase of our relationship was very difficult, as there were many rough edges that had to be worked out. A lot of this had to do with the guilt Little was also feeling about her marriage ending. But as we worked out many of our personal ego beliefs, our relationship began to blossom in a very deep and beautiful way.

She was the love and light of my life. She was my best friend and she was a teacher for me in so many ways. She was the happiest person I have ever known. She radiated light which attracted many people to her. In the last few years of our earthly relationship, I felt as if we had become one person. My love for her was so deep there was nothing I wouldn't have done for her. Little retired at the age of 56 and had almost 14 years to do the many things she wanted to do before her sudden death in 2010. I retired four years after Little and we were very blessed in that we had nine and a half years of retirement together, during which time we went on many great trips and enjoyed so many wonderful parts of the world together.

In the last few years of her life she became thoroughly involved in Japanese tea ceremony and learning the Japanese language. They were both difficult for her, but as with everything she did, she put her heart and soul into it. She told me many times that she felt like a little child playing a game when she was doing the tea ceremony. Learning Japanese was very difficult for her, but she loved and enjoyed it so much. She would study Japanese for two to four hours a day. One of the reasons she was so driven to learn both of these things was because of a Japanese woman we met on a trip we took to Egypt in 1999. The woman was a Japanese tea ceremony teacher and she and Little became extremely close. Little went to Japan to visit her and her husband four or five times and they also came to our house for several visits.

Deep personal love can create an opening of the heart center, which is the doorway through which Divine Love can enter this world. This happened to me in my relationship with my partner. Through her life and then her death, Little played an invaluable part in the opening of my heart, which allowed me to open up to receiving Divine Love.

On April 29th of 2010 at 6:46 in the morning, Little initially left her body. I had just finished meditating and went upstairs to have breakfast. I heard a groan in the bathroom and I ran in. Little told me she wasn't feeling well and asked me to help her to bed. I walked her the few feet to the bed and laid her down. I noticed she took a labored breath and I immediately called 911. She took one more short breath and left her body. I knew she had left but it was such a shock that it did not register in my consciousness. I was looking at her while I was talking to the 911 operator and I could not believe what had just happened. A few seconds ago I was helping her to bed and now she was gone. She had always been the picture of health. We both were in great physical shape. She had just turned 69 years old a month earlier, but she looked much, much younger. People who met her for the first time could not believe her age. We went hiking just about every day. She very rarely ever got tired.

The 911 operator contacted the paramedics who arrived at our house very quickly and had to use the defibrillation paddles to get her heart beating again. That day, they had to use the paddles three different times to restart her heart. Little was taken to the Intensive Care Unit, but she never regained consciousness. Three days later, on Sunday, May 2nd at 4:17 in the morning, Little took her final breath and left this world. The cause of death was a massive blood clot that had apparently come up from her leg and went to the lungs where it cut off all oxygen to the heart and other organs. The doctors said a condition like that is usually caused by a trauma to the body, but I could not think of any injuries to her body in the last number of years before her death.

Despite all my years of spiritual work and my knowing that our separation was an illusion, I was completely devastated. I went home that Sunday and in the evening I sat down to try and meditate. I had only slept an hour on Thursday and Friday and not at all on Saturday. I didn't know if I would be able to meditate as my body was in such deep shock, but I didn't know what else to do. As soon as I closed my eyes, I was filled with a beautiful white light. I immediately felt Little's presence stronger than I had ever felt it while she was in a body. I saw an image of an energy field and she was one part of it and I was the other half. I then saw myself traveling at a great speed through a tunnel made of light. I could also see stars in the distance. While I was in this tunnel I was shown an image of my heart. My heart was made of white light and I was half the heart and Little was the other half. This light heart was then superimposed over my physical heart. During this time I could feel a lot of activity in my physical heart. My meditation lasted about an hour and during this time I felt absolutely no sense of loss or separation. Quite the contrary, I had never felt such a union with Little as I did during my meditation. This meditation was an amazing blessing I received on the day of her departure and I am extremely grateful for that experience.

I want to interject something here about the term Twin Flames or Twin Souls. My experience in the meditation I just described might lead someone to think that Little and I were part of the same soul. This is not what a Twin Flame or Twin Soul is. Each individual soul contains both the feminine and masculine aspect within itself, so there is nobody we need to seek to make us whole. A Twin Flame is the soul that was the closest to us when we were first birthed as an individual being, sort of like identical twins. Astrology uses the time and place of birth and how the other planets, sun and moon were in relationship to the location of your birth as a way to create your chart. The way all the energies of that moment would be influencing that particular location at the time of birth would allow the astrologer to determine the path of the soul. Imagine identical twins being birth at the same exact moment. It would be hard for an astrologer to give any variance as to what may happen to each twin at any given time, unless the astrologer was using her intuition.

A soul is made of a positive force and negative force. The positive force manifests as a male when it enters the earth plane and the negative force is suppressed. The negative force manifests as a female with the positive force being suppressed. As a soul develops he becomes more balanced in the polarities and eventually both the positive and negative forces come into perfect balance and are expressing equally through a body. A male will still be a male and a female will still be a female but in perfect balance of expression.

A twin soul is the soul that was closest to us at the time that our Mother God gave birth to us at the beginning of our individuation. There is no one who could be more like us than our twin soul and yet there is a difference. Each of us is whole and complete and unique in our own way. We have to let go of the idea that any person is needed to make us whole. Most of us will meet our twin soul as we are reaching the end of our journey in this illusionary world. Our twin soul can be of immense help in creating what it is we came to do on earth, as we can for them. I do not know at this time if Little is my twin soul, but if not, she certainly was a very powerful soul mate.

After Little left her body I went through a very deep and sometimes very dark grieving process. One morning, seventeen days after Little's departure, I woke up feeling a very heavy darkness hanging over me. I call the experience I had on this day, 'my darkest day'. I had experienced darkness before, but this feeling was something much stronger than I had ever experienced. I thought that if I were to get out in nature the feeling of darkness might lessen, so I went for a long walk at one of the lakes near our house. Being out in nature did not seem to help, in fact the darkness I was experiencing just kept getting darker. I went home and around four o'clock that afternoon the dark experience completely took me over. I experienced a state of darkness completely devoid of light or hope of any sort. It was an experience of absolute hopelessness and lifelessness. The only thing I could think of doing at the time was to go downstairs to my meditation room and just try and observe what was happening. I was at the top of the stairs getting ready to go downstairs when the darkest of the dark experience just seemed to take over. Tears began pouring out of my eyes and without even thinking about it, the words, "I don't even know who I am" came out of my mouth three times. It is impossible to describe the dark and lifeless state I was experiencing. If I believed in hell, this would have been the darkest place in hell. I felt that going any further into the darkness would have resulted in total non-existence. That is how dark it was. It is as though I had gone to the very edge of darkness, touched it and then turned around. I am thankful that the most intense part of the experience only lasted about 20 minutes. During the experience I could feel a lot of activity in my heart. As I was experiencing the darkness, I experienced being conscious on three different levels. The first level was of me experiencing this darkness. The next level was more of my normal conscious state. On this level I was very surprised at the words coming out of my mouth because I was totally confident of my spiritual identity. The third level was the observer state. The observer is usually very neutral and non-emotional when watching events in our life, but even the observer was really surprised at the intensity of darkness that the first level was experiencing.

During this experience I intuitively knew that I was facing, what Eckhart Tolle refers to, in his book 'The Power of Now' as the pain body. You can look at the pain body as a separate entity that dwells within us and is made up of all our accumulated pain, guilt and fear through many life times. The pain body is activated by situations that it resonates with. If anger is a big part of our pain body, then any situation which causes us anger will most likely activate the pain body within us. The loss of Little activated my pain body at the deepest level. The death of my mother, the loss of family and the feelings of separation I experienced as a child and probably other lifetimes, were all part of that pain body which manifested on this day. The loss of Little also triggered the deepest pain of all, the pain of the seeming separation from God. The seeming separation from God is by far the deepest and most painful of all. The pain body is part of the ego structure. On the 'darkest day', I experienced a death of my ego on a very deep level.

Many years ago, before I had ever heard about the pain body, I intuitively knew that when my pain body was being activated that I was to observe the feeling I was experiencing, without any judgment or identification, just simply to watch it. This observation, without judgment or interpretation, starts to dissolve the pain body. When I was going through the dark experience I just described, I was not even thinking about observing it because of the overwhelming power of the experience. Fortunately, because I had practiced this technique over many years, the observer state was there automatically. One of the greatest gifts we can give ourselves when we are in pain of any kind is to observe the pain as it arises in us without any judgment or resistance. Allow it to be as though it was giving us a message. As we allow it to deliver its message, we are allowing a certain part of our pain body to dissolve. We can use our current pain to help dissolve all our accumulated pain. The pain could manifest as a simple state of impatience, or it could be a state of suicidal depression. Neither of these states has anything to do with who we are, but if we identify with these feelings as part of our self, we are giving life and power to an illusion which will cause us even more pain and in extreme cases, the taking of our own life.

Obviously I got through the day and the next morning I got up feeling very light. I knew that I had released some very deep pain having to do with the feeling of being abandoned. It took something of the magnitude of Little's departure to bring this up and release it. This was definitely not the end of my grieving over the loss of her as I had a couple of years of deep grieving after she left. Her departure opened the way for the greater purification and opening of my heart. This was one of the many gifts I received over time as a result of her departure. During many of my meditations after her departure, I felt her presence so strongly that I began talking to her just as if she were in a physical body. In a few meditations I felt her presence very strongly and opened my eyes and saw her as an oval sphere of white light. I knew she was working very closely with me. I still miss her physical presence immensely, but I have now developed a strong relationship with her in spirit. Shortly after her departure I found out that she had become one of my spirit guides, so our relationship still continues to get stronger even though she is not in a physical body.

So many synchronicities happened shortly before Little left her body, that I knew this event was definitely orchestrated from above and was something

Little and I had agreed upon before entering the earth. The night before she left I asked her if she would like to see a video and she said yes, so I went to the video store. I was trying to read the synopsis of a particular video I wanted to pick up, but for some reason I could not read it so I put it back. I was then led to a video on the new release shelf. I went over and immediately picked up the video and took it home. The name of the video is 'Love Happens'. Maybe some of you have seen it. It is a very cute movie with Jennifer Anniston and Aaron Eckhart. While we were watching the movie, Little commented a few times of how much she loved the movie. One of the main themes of the movie is the extreme necessity of fully grieving the loss of a loved one in order to fully heal and come out the other side even stronger. I could not even conceive of the idea, while watching the movie, that in a matter of a few hours the message of the movie was to be a very important lesson for me over the next couple of years. I never could have imagined that just 9 hours after watching the movie that she would be leaving this earth. I thought about the movie quite often as I was going through a grieving process which propelled me on an even faster spiritual journey.

I know that on some level we were both aware that she would be leaving. I say this because of some of the things that happened shortly before she left. Two nights before her departure we were sitting on the bed when out of the clear, Little said, "You know Gilbert, that one of us is going to leave first and leave the other behind." I replied, "I don't know Little, maybe we will both leave together." She then said, "No Gilbert, one of us is going to leave first and leave the other behind." I responded, "Well Little, I really don't think about stuff like that." Little then said, "Well, I just hope I go first." Two days later she was gone.

On the last full day of her life on earth, she had an appointment with a physical therapist in Calistoga, which is about a 1 ½ hour drive from where we lived. She had been to the therapist many times before and had always gone alone, unless I also had an appointment with the same therapist. Little visited different therapist to keep her body finely tuned. She had been having some pain in her right leg and was going to see the therapist in Calistoga about it. We both thought it was sciatica, but as it turned out it was a blood clot which eventually caused her death. The morning of her appointment I woke up and knew that I had to drive her to her appointment. I went upstairs after meditation and asked her if she would like me to drive her to the appointment. She was very surprised at the offer and quickly said yes. On a deeper level I knew this was her last day and I wanted to spend every second with her. Thankfully, as a protective measure, this knowledge did not filter down to my conscious mind. A number of other things like this happened in the last few days of her life which made me aware that on some level we both knew what was going to happen. We had agreed to this whole scenario before we even came into the body. We are now working together to complete the mission we were sent to fulfill.

The grieving process I went through was one of my final lessons on my spiritual journey on my path to Christ Consciousness. My heart went through a greater purification and awakening because of this grieving process. Little was a major factor in bringing about the expansion of my heart and I have thanked her over and over again. My heart was so closed for most of my life because of the pain that I experienced as a child. She did something for me, which for the majority of my life seemed impossible. She opened my heart completely and for that I will be eternally grateful to her. It's almost as if she gave up her physical life in order to accelerate my spiritual development.

My meditation experience on the day of her departure caused me to do research on the subject of twin souls. I found a great book on the internet entitled 'Twin Flames' by Antera, a woman who lives in Mt. Shasta with her twin flame husband, Omaran. They are a beautiful couple who are doing very important spiritual work for the world. I visited them many times over the next several years and received a lot of healing through my association with them. Omaran was directed by an ascended master to build a pyramid on their property. Omaran had been a contractor and was given the directions and dimensions of how to build the pyramid. I have spent many hours in the Mt. Shasta pyramid and I can tell you that it is very powerful.

There is one thing that we all need to know about love between people. We can never truly be loved by another unless we love ourselves. It is the law of cause and effect. I have stated a number of times that everything that seems to be happening in the world is happening in our minds. What we are experiencing is what we believe about the world and ourselves. If we don't believe we are loveable, no one can reach us with their love no matter how hard they try. The love we are looking for through another must first be found in ourselves. People might think that infatuation or possession is a form of love but it is not true love and will only create problems between people. There's a country western song entitled 'Looking for Love'. In the lyrics of the song there is a phrase which goes like this: 'Looking for love in all the wrong places, looking for love in too many faces.' This is exactly what I did a good portion of my life and what the great majority of the world is doing. We think we are going to fill the hole in ourselves through the love and attention of another. We're looking in the wrong place. We can't take another persons' love and make it our own. That won't fulfill us. We need to find the love that is deep within our own heart. This love within us will bring us fulfillment in just about everything we do. Then if we do come together with another who is in a similar state, it would probably be a very beautiful relationship.

In conclusion to this chapter, I am inserting a couple of pictures of Little to show my appreciation for the amazing part she played in my life. Both of the pictures were taken one or two years prior to Little leaving her body.

Pictured below is Little feeding deer out side of our house

Pictured above, Little having her morning Japanese green tea

CHAPTER 5

Free Will or Destiny

The question of whether our experiences here on earth are predestined, or a result of our choices, is a philosophical question that has been pondered throughout history. Many astrologers say that a person with many planets in fixed signs in their chart, have less of a choice as to what their path may be. These fixed aspects may be in the chart of a soul who has created a lot of karma and now needs to start paying off some of that debt. He therefore has, by karmic necessity, taken on a more restricted path in that life. Fixed aspects in the chart of a very highly evolved soul are for the purpose of fulfilling a particular purpose the soul chose to take on in that lifetime. Yet in both cases, there is the element of free will which can always change the direction of the life. A person experiencing a more restricted life, because of karma, would have less use of his free will, but as long as we are in the world of duality and have free will, anything is possible.

I came into this life with the intention of taking on the fullness of the Christ Consciousness and fulfilling whatever spiritual purpose it was I came to do. I have wondered at times whether I could have stepped off my spiritual path and gone on a different and darker journey because of the difficulties I faced in life. I really can't say. I have known some very spiritually evolved beings who had a lot of light but had not fully relinquished their ego and thus made choices which led them down some dark paths.

There are also very highly evolved souls that chose to take on very difficult experiences in life in order to take on some of the karma of the world. In this realm of duality, it is even possible for these highly evolved souls to lose their way because of the difficult path they chose. Think of the amazing love and courage these souls have for humanity.

In one of his trance sessions, Edgar Cayce said, "A man's will creates his destiny." This is more along the lines of my thinking regarding 'free will or destiny'. I mentioned earlier that in my experiences in the Holy Order of Mans, there was such a strong ego pull to leave the Order in that first year, that it took every ounce of my will to stay the course. Was it predestined that I should stay, or was it free will? There obviously are some predestined experiences in each of our lives because of karma and choice, but it is the free will of an individual which determine whether these experiences become something greater or lesser.

Many souls come into the earth under extremely difficult circumstances because of past karma, but even these difficulties can be transcended through the use of the will. There is a saying, 'Know that at any time, free will can draw the sword out of the stone'. That is how powerful our will is. It comes down to how much we want something and how far are we willing to apply our self to get it.

For those of you familiar with the tarot deck, there is a card entitled 'Wheel of Fortune' which represents the cycle of birth, death and rebirth in this dream world. Some lifetimes will be easier than others, but we will continue to ride the wheel of fortune with all its ups and downs, until we make a decision to wake up and get off the karmic cycle. As long as we believe that the individual we seem to be is our true identity and that we are separate from God, our lives are in a sense predestined. We will continue to ride the roller coaster of life, with all its ups and downs until we decide that we have had enough. The greatest tool that we have at our disposal to get off the wheel of birth and death is our freedom of choice. The power of our will can not only change our present, but our past and future as well. Our destiny is in our hands.

As our understanding of truth grows, we will realize the futility of blaming someone else for anything that happens in our life. We will know that the outer events taking place in our lives, are really taking place in our mind and that everything in our mind is our creation and our responsibility. If we continue to allow the ego to choose our path in life, we will continue on the treadmill of birth and death, with the fear of death being paramount in our minds.

Even if you travel the spiritual path you will still end up dying, won't you?

A person who has spiritually awakened will also leave the body behind, but his experience of death will be incredibly beautiful. Leaving his body will be like stepping out of a car which has served its purpose. A spiritually awakened person will also have broken the cycle of birth and death and will no longer need to reincarnate in this world, although she may decide to incarnate again to help humanity. She will not experience fear when she does leave her body, because she knows that there is no such thing as death. In fact her experience will be one of joy. Unfortunately, most people experience death with fear, dread and usually a lot of pain.

As we begin taking control of our destiny through our spiritual striving, the difficult astrological influences which we were born with can be transcended. We are the creators of our destiny, not the planets. We are also creators of the stars, not their servants.

In order to understand how free will and destiny both have their place in this illusionary world, I will explain something. When the separation from God first occurred in the mind of the Son of God, it created a great deal of guilt and fear. These emotions set the stage for the creation of the false ego. The ego promised us a way out of our feelings of guilt and a new and better life. We accepted the ego's will and direction without questioning the ego's insane logic. The ego's insane logic, based on fear, will continue to create our destiny until we have made the choice to wake up. The ego's desire for everyone in this world is for us to remain asleep so it can maintain control. The masses of people are like robots, or hypnotized subjects, blindly following the insane plan of the ego. I will expound on this idea in greater detail later in this chapter.

We have within us the power to choose truth over illusion. We can choose to follow the path of awakening with the Holy Spirit as our guide. In the beginning of the spiritual path, we simply need to have a willingness to find out what the Truth is. As we grow spiritually through our choices and efforts, our life and path will change accordingly. A person who makes this new choice is now moving away from the insane script of the ego and moving towards a new script which will lead to the peace that we all seek.

Once a person makes the decision that he wants truth above all, his predestined life can be altered drastically. As we learn to be guided by truth, we take control of our destiny which will eventually bring us to our spiritual awakening. No matter how deeply enmeshed in illusion we are, we always have the choice to extricate ourselves from the darkness of this illusionary world.

How can we choose the Holy Spirit as our guide, instead of the ego?

When you wake up in the morning, have the intention that you will allow the Holy Spirit to make all decisions for you in that day. Anytime you have a decision to make, silently ask the Holy Spirit to guide you in making the correct choice. Anytime you are in a situation in which you feel any type of upset, offer the situation to the Holy Spirit so that a negative situation can be turned into a positive one. Make it a habit to bring the Holy Spirit into all your affairs. As you do this you will find your life becoming much brighter and more peaceful. You are silently turning your life over to a force that is incapable of error. You are turning your life over to the Will of God.

There is one thing I am happy to report that is absolutely predestined for each and every one of us. We will all eventually regain our full awareness of our unity with God. There is nothing we can do that will change that outcome, although we can choose to remain asleep and continue in a state of illusion, pain and separation for as long as we desire. God has placed no time limit as to when we choose to awaken.

Karma is a word that has become very popular in the last 50 years. Scientifically the word can be described as the law of cause and effect: for every action there is an equal and opposite reaction. Jeshua said, "What a man sows, so shall he reap" which is another way to describe the law of karma. This law could be called the universal balance scale which always keeps the author and his creation in perfect balance. The conditions of our life, work, finances, mental and emotional states are all a result of how we have used this law in the past. We activate the law of cause and effect through our beliefs, desires and most importantly our will. Our life experiences are simply a manifestation of our beliefs, desires and choices through the law of cause and effect. The law of cause and effect does not take into consideration the person who is using it. This law simply produces the effects of what we think and believe.

Was our destiny determined at the time we were created by God?

Our destiny began after we seemed to separate from God and entered the ego stage. It was then that we started using our free will to determine our destiny. How and why particular individualities came into being, I do not know. We were always there as a possibility and at some point that possibility manifested as us. It is the nature of love to continually create and expand. We are literally an extension of God with all the attributes, creativeness and power of God. We are one with God. At a certain point in creation, we were birthed by God. Not all souls were birthed at the same time. This birthing process took place in waves. Some souls are much older than others, which in no way makes them better or superior. Yet in most cases these older souls are much closer to enlightenment than the younger ones because of their greater experience.

As spiritual children we were one with God and His creation, creating and extending Gods' creation as co-creators. As spiritual adolescents some of us fell asleep and seemed to go our own way. Because of our having fallen asleep, we have forgotten our unity with God. In spiritual maturity we return to the state of unity with God, referred to as the return of the prodigal son. We return to God with much greater wisdom and light than when we left because we return with a new state of consciousness. Because of our expansion into Christ Consciousness, we have added a new aliveness to the creation of God.

When we fell asleep, we actually believed that the separation from God was real. Now remember, we were created in the image of God and our thoughts have unlimited powers. This belief in the separation from God created a conundrum. Separation could not possibly happen in God's kingdom where all is one. There was only one place this idea could manifest and that was in a realm of unreality as in a very deep sleep. When we dream at night we enter a realm of mind called the sub-conscious. The term sub-conscious means below the threshold of consciousness, in other words - unconsciousness. This illusionary dream world here on earth is a realm of unconsciousness where the great majority of people are asleep and unaware of what is real. They believe that this dream world is their reality. The spiritual path is a process of awakening from this dream.

As we fell into a deep sleep in an imaginary world of illusion, we gradually lost memory of who we were and of our connection to God. In this illusionary world, the belief in the ideas of separation, individuality, good and evil, and suffering came into being. This is the symbolism of Adam and Eve eating of the tree of the knowledge of good and evil and being cast out of the Garden of Eden. A spiritual aspirant's task is to use his free will to awaken from this dream.

Even in this confused world, our judicial system has compassionate laws which protect insane people from punishment for crimes they committed without their full mental faculties. If this illusionary world knows enough to have compassion on others who are not in their right minds, why do we insist on condemning ourselves for a bad dream?

The world believes in time and a linear progression of events, when in fact this unreality happened in an instant in our mind and then was over. We are repeatedly living the memories of this instant over and over in our minds. We cling to this illusion as our reality and seem to suffer, die and be born again. By clinging to guilt, false beliefs and desires, we sentence ourselves to continuing cycles of births and deaths in a place that doesn't exist. When we are finally tired enough of all this pain, we seek a way out. Except for those who have awakened, there is no real joy in this world. There are fleeting distractions from our desperate states, but no real lasting joy. Through our free will we can change our destiny from one of desperation into one of total peace.

I now want to ask you a series of questions. Should we condemn a child for having a bad dream? Should the child be forced to feel guilty for a dream over which he had no control? Should children fear their parents because of a bad dream? Should children be forced to spend time in a place called purgatory, or even worse hell, because of a silly dream? Actually our fears and guilt have created places like purgatory and hell but it was we who have condemned ourselves to these places, not some judgmental God. The great spiritual teachers of the past and present told us that we must wake up from this dream, that we must change our way of thinking and realize that in reality we are children of the Most High? Buddha taught that everything in this world is temporary and subject to decay and therefore could not be real. Jeshua said that we shall know the truth and the truth will set us free. We cannot be forced to accept truth, just as a horse can be led to water but not forced to drink. It is just a matter of whether we are tired enough of being afraid of so many things which seem to be out of our control, that we start looking for something with greater meaning and lasting reward.

When a soul comes to the full realization that this life is just a dream, it doesn't mean she has the license to do whatever she wants and be able to get away with it. We still have to abide by the universal law of cause and effect and what we create we must experience. The realization that this world is all a dream also does not mean we have overcome the world. We have to choose the process of remembering who we are so that we can accept the oneness of all that is. Remember that as long as we maintain a belief in separation, we are bound by that belief and will continue to return to earth until we realize the truth. By seeing the perfection in every person and situation we encounter throughout the day we open the door to our own perfection. As we do this, we will begin to realize the illusion of the world we seem to live in. We are exchanging illusion for reality. This is a process that will take some time. Our willingness and vigilance to completely reverse our belief system will help immeasurably in shortening the amount of time it will take us to wake up. Each soul has free will and it is through our will that we determine our direction and experiences of life.

Imagine that you were sentenced to prison for 20 years and the judge told you that your sentence would be reduced by one year for every 40 hours of hard labor you performed in the prison. I don't think there are too many of us who wouldn't put in at least 40, 80 or more hours a week in order to get out of prison as soon as possible. The problem that most of us have is that we don't realize that we are in a prison. We are so asleep that we believe the life we seem to be living is the way it is supposed to be. Those of us who know that this is not the life we were intended to live will do everything in our power to choose to awaken each and every moment of every day.

What about a person who has accumulated a lot of negative karma, does a person like this still have to pay off all his karma before he can awaken?

Is it necessary to experience all the negative results of the karma we have created? The answer is no, although the karmic scale must be balanced. This balancing can be fulfilled through good deeds. If we understand the truth and are sincere in forgiving ourselves and others for false beliefs and actions, we can transcend the negative karma we have created. Remember, none of this is real so how hard can it be to let go of illusion? True forgiveness is the key.

Buddha taught that it is imperative to seek true understanding, because only then can we begin the process of releasing the shackles of illusion that bind us. Truth is only realized by a mind willing to let go of its old beliefs and ways of doing things in order to make room for a much greater light.

We must come to the realization that we have been tricked by the ego into believing a complete lie. I want to repeat that we don't have to sacrifice anything to God to atone for what we did because this just validates the illusion of sin. We simply need to be sincere in our desire to know the truth which will lead us to the awakening. Knowing the truth will open the way for us to forgive ourselves and the whole world for things that seemed to have happened in a dream. It was never real.

I've talked to many people who seem to think the world is getting worse and not better and outwardly this may appear to be so. The spiritual awakening that I am referring to consists of a greater spiritual awareness which is being realized by many individuals who are having profound effects on the mind of this world. We are all connected and what one thinks in India affects the minds of all people because of our shared consciousness. Beliefs in Illusion have power because they are believed by Sons of God. Take a look at the world and what we have created and this will give you an indication of how powerful our thoughts are. Many years ago I read a book entitled 'The Science of Mind' by Ernest Holmes. It really helped me to understand the importance of being very aware of what I was thinking. One sentence in the book pretty much summed up the essence of the message of the book. That sentence was, **"To learn how to think is to learn how to live."**

Powerful spiritual thoughts have tremendous influence on the mind of this world. Most of us have no idea of the power of our thoughts. The printing of A Course in Miracles and other spiritually inspired books have made the truth available to all mankind. A sincere seeker needs only to use their free will and apply the principles in these books to begin their awakening process. Even in this day and age most people are not ready to know the truth. They are so identified with the ego that the truth is a threat to their illusionary existence. The ego knows that truth will dispel all illusion and thus end it's illusionary existence. There is absolutely no judgment of a soul if he chooses to remain asleep. We are all at different stages of spiritual development and what may be right for Jim may be wrong for Joe. The spiritual path is for those souls who are seeking a much greater and more fulfilling life. All souls will eventually travel this path.

Here's another short story I made up that allows us to look at the world's situation in another way. A large ship sailing from a very wealthy country was captured by the military of a small dictatorial country. The thousands of people aboard the ship were put in prison. Years passed and the captives endured a daily life of pain, drudgery and hopelessness. Many prisoners became so accustomed to prison life that they actually believed they were content. When word about the hijack and kidnapping finally reached the king of the wealthy country, he sent his best troops to infiltrate the country which was ruled by a dictator. These troops landed in the dead of night and by the next morning had taken on the dress and manners of the foreigners in order to blend in and not be detected. Slowly these special troops began to infiltrate positions of power in the country and eventually, one was appointed as warden of the prison. The new warden appointed many of the other special troops as guards. When all positions of importance in the prison were under the authority of the special troops, word was passed to all the prisoners that several ships from their country were on the way to rescue them.

Amazingly some of the prisoners had completely forgotten about their homeland and paid no attention to those who had come to rescue them. Others listened at first but then became so caught up in their routine that the message was soon forgotten. But many were overjoyed at the news and started preparing for their escape. No one knew when the ships would arrive, not even the warden. About a day before the ships were to arrive, the warden received word through a special transmission. He sent the guards into the prison to tell the inmates to get ready to leave as soon as he gave the word. Some of the inmates who had forgotten their homeland and were content to be in the prison threatened to tell the dictator about this plan, but since they could not get out of the prison grounds, it was an empty threat. The following morning at sunrise the ships arrived and all the inmates willing to go back to their country were loaded aboard. The warden and the guards tried to talk some sense into the remaining inmates telling them about the beauty and the joy of their country, but the unconscious inmates would not listen and continue to threaten to tell the dictator. Finally the warden and the guards realized it was too late and sadly had to leave their remaining country men in this dark prison because of their refusal to leave.

It was our free will which seemingly allowed us to create the unimaginable. Our choice caused us to fall asleep and believe that we had separated ourselves from God. It is this same power of choice which will allow us to once again awaken to our holy union with God.

Truth is understood on many different levels according to a person's spiritual development. We constantly have the freedom to choose between truth and illusion. I will now seemingly contradict myself by saying that in **reality** there is no such thing as a will which is separate from God's Will. The key word here is **reality**. When we reach a certain state of spiritual development, we will come to the realization that there is truly only one Will and that is the Will of God. We were created in the image and likeness of God and by our very nature, our true will is absolutely the same as the Will of God. When we become so disillusioned with our lives, and begin our spiritual journey, we will begin to get glimpses of this amazing truth.

You keep saying that what I am experiencing is not really taking place? I can feel the pain and I know it is real.

I agree that it does seem to be very real and can seem to be agonizing until we begin to awaken. Our minds seem to be split. One part of our mind, which is controlled by the false ego, causes us to fully believe in the illusion and drama of this world. The other part of our mind, which is our true self, is patiently waiting until we start calling upon it for help. Once we have made the decision to wake up, the true part of our mind will begin to slowly dissolve the ego mind, just as the sun dissipates the darkness when it begins to rise at dawn. Is it Free Will or Destiny? Both have tremendous implications in our lives but free will triumphs over destiny in the sense that through the focused use of our will, we can change our destiny. The question is whether we are going to choose to use the unlimited power of our will to change our destiny?

Prayer

Throughout my spiritual journey, there was one prayer which was always on the tip of my tongue. The prayer I am referring to is: "Be it unto me according to Your Will Mother/Father God". It was a light for me in my darkest hours and a healing balm when my soul was enduring many challenges. It was the staff I needed to lean on when ascending some of the rougher peaks of the spiritual mountain. It was a lighthouse when I encountered stormy seas. This prayer has been a sacred mantra for me. As I mentioned before, my first year in the Holy Order of Mans was immensely difficult. I wanted to leave the Order so often because of the mental, emotional and physical discomfort I experienced. Each time I had this intense desire to leave I would go to the chapel and pray that God's Will and not my own be done. This prayer and my willingness to do God's Will allowed me to go through this process of transformation.

This particular prayer may not resonate with the way many of you pray and that is perfectly fine. Just find your own way of seeking God's Will in your life. We are all unique and have our own way of communicating with our Creator. When we experience that sacred state where we consciously commune with God, our spirit will flow through us and the perfect words will naturally come out of our mouth without any thought. When his disciples asked Jeshua how to pray, he gave them the Lords' prayer. In this prayer he states "Thy Will be done on earth as it is in heaven." Just talk from your heart when you pray to God and you will be heard. In our prayers, we can surrender all our worries and problems and accept that our mind be healed which can bring us great comfort. Praying is an intimate way of communing with our true Mother/Father. When you begin to make that intimate connection with God in prayer your own higher self will do the talking and you will feel the bliss of that sacred communion. The important thing in prayer is our willingness to surrender our individual will to the One Will that governs all that is. We are one with God and so God's Will is our will. In surrendering to God's Will, we are surrendering to the truth of who we are. As I began to let go of my personal will my prayers became much more powerful. I felt the strong connection to God each time I would raise my consciousness towards Her in prayer. It was such a beautiful and blissful feeling that tears would start pouring down my face. I now understand how some saints would levitate during prayer because of the strong connection with God.

True prayer comes from the sincerity and devotion in the heart of the one saying the prayer. It is very difficult to have a deep connection with God in prayer if we perceive Him as someone who is so far beyond our reach, so far above us. We need to speak to God in a personal way as a child would speak to her mother whom she knows loves her unconditionally. If we are truly sincere in our prayer and speak from the heart, God will answer us. That answer may come in the form of an inner voice or through something someone else says to us. The answer may also come in the form of a situation that appears in our life. God will be personal to us if we are personal to Her. We can tell Him our deepest yearnings and concerns if we accept Him in a personal way. A personal relationship with God allows us to fully open our hearts in prayer. God dwells within the heart of every individual, so we cannot have a much closer, personal and intimate a relationship with anybody.

Our personal communication with God is extremely beautiful, but there is another type of prayer. This type of prayer is reflected in the way we live our lives. How do we treat others regardless of their status in this world? How do we respond to the good fortune and difficulties that we encounter in life? A living prayer is a constant prayer without ceasing. If we live our lives in the best and highest way we know how, then we become a living prayer. I think the simplest and best way to depict a living prayer is through a story that came to me in the last couple of days. This story is filled with symbolism of the journey that all light workers have chosen to take.

Once upon a time very high up in the mountains there was a beautiful kingdom where the people lived a very loving and joyous life. The king was very loving and kind and treated all his subjects as though each one were his own son or daughter. The kingdom got its water from melting snow from the highest peak of the mountain. One day someone discovered that the water coming down the mountain was contaminated and not totally pure so he brought it to the attention of the king. The king called together his wisest advisors and asked what could be done to purify the water as he did not want his subjects to get sick. After much deliberation the advisors told the king that there was only one element that could purify the water and that was gold. The only problem was that there was no gold available in the kingdom or on the mountain on which they lived. One of the advisors told the king that he had a vision of a place way down in the valley where a dragon lived guarding a very large golden egg. The advisor added that in his vision he was shown that the valley was very dark and filled with many dangers and the powerful dragon would kill anyone who came close to the golden egg. The advisor also warned the king that it was possible that anyone going to the valley might completely forget all about the kingdom and their identity because of the perils and darkness in the valley.

The king went into deep contemplation and then called together his twelve most courageous and devoted warriors and asked if they would volunteer to go into the valley and bring back the golden egg. He told them about the immense dangers in the valley and that because of the darkness down there, there was a strong probability that they would temporarily forget who they were and why they were even in the valley. He told them the light in their hearts would always be a guiding voice to lead them home and to pay close attention to that voice. The king told them that the journey he was sending them on would be very difficult but that he knew they would succeed. The twelve warriors loved the king with all their hearts and agreed to take on this mission. After a huge celebration, they were sent off by the king and the subjects of the kingdom with deep gratitude and love.

Once the warriors reached the depth of the valley, the darkness started to take its toll. They all began to forget who they were and why they were in this strange place, but they continued on together even though they did not know where they were going. The first group of people the warriors encountered were from a small village and the villagers invited the warriors to eat with them. The warriors were very hungry and the food was so delicious that one of the warriors decided to live with the villagers and learn all he could about cooking.

So the eleven continued on with their journey and the next village they came upon was inhabited by the most beautiful women they could imagine. One of the warriors was so enticed by the beauty of the women that he decided to live in the village. Now there were only ten warriors left and they continued their journey, not really knowing where they were going or for what reason. The next group of natives the warriors encountered were fierce warriors and again one of the warriors chose to stay and learn the skills of war. Later on they came to a village where the villagers were expert in black magic and again one of the warriors chose to stay and learn this art. Over time the warriors came across other villages which enticed some of the warriors to stay.

Over the next year the group of warriors became smaller and smaller as one by one they became enamored with different facets of life in the valley. Finally there was only one warrior left and his name was Christopher. Christopher was the bravest of all the warriors and because of his dedication the voice within his heart began to speak to him. He slowly started to remember more and more about his purpose for coming into the valley. At that point of his journey, Christopher started encountering more and more people who directed him and told him about a large one hundred foot tall dragon who lived in a cave. They also told him about the huge golden egg the dragon was protecting.

As Christopher continued his journey he actually began to hear the loud roar of the dragon in the distance. At that point, he no longer encountered anyone as they were all too afraid to get close to where the dragon lived. He had to travel the last part of the journey alone. As Christopher continued on the road he was travelling, the roar of the dragon became louder and louder so that even Christopher began to experience fear. Even through the fear he was experiencing, the voice of guidance within him became louder and clearer and told him to be courageous and no harm would come to him. This voice gave Christopher the courage to go on but he still had no idea how one man could possibly kill a dragon of that size, but now that he clearly remembered his purpose he was determined to try and get the egg for his king and the people of the kingdom.

Then one morning as Christopher walked over a little hill he saw the large dark cave where the dragon lived. Great fear filled his heart as the roar of the dragon was almost deafening. The voice within him told him to keep moving past any fear that might arise. The only thing that kept Christopher going was his desire to fulfill his king's request. With sword in hand, Christopher entered the dark cave. He had never experienced fear in the kingdom but now it was so encompassing that he found it hard to walk and yet he found the courage to continue moving forward. He could now sense the heat from the dragon's breath. Christopher knew that around the next corner he would face his greatest fear and challenge. His great heart was beating so fast that he had difficulty breathing. His courage was now being tested to the fullest. Knowing that there would be a good chance that he was going to be killed by the dragon Christopher courageously stepped around the corner to face the dragon. To his utter amazement there was no dragon or golden egg. Then out of the blue in a flash of illumination, Christopher realized that because of his willingness to face his greatest fear for the sake of others, he had become the gold that he was seeking and which the kingdom needed to purify the contaminated waters. It was through his dedication and willingness to die to fulfill the king's edict that he was transformed into the very essence of what he was seeking. In great joy and ecstasy, Christopher sat down in the cave and realized that the king had known all along that this was the true purpose of this journey. With that understanding he began laughing harder and longer than he had ever laughed before. By honoring the king's request above all else, an inner transformation had occurred within him and he now carried a new consciousness which had been missing in the kingdom before his journey. Because of his courage and devotion, he had opened a way for the water in the kingdom to be purified and for all in the kingdom to have an even more expansive and glorious life. Christopher was lovingly greeted by the king and all the subjects and the greatest of all feasts was held in his honor.

I have written this book with the intention of reaching light workers who are just waking up. Each of the twelve warriors represents an aspect of the light workers journey. Initially they got lost in the darkness and enticements of the world. They eventually reach the Christopher stage and are ready to fulfill the purpose for which they initially entered the journey of duality. They are ready to live their lives as a living prayer. I will explain the symbolism and purpose of the journey of light workers through the earth plane, represented by the twelve warriors, in much greater detail in Chapter 12. The main point I wanted to make with this story is that our greatest prayer to God is reflected in the way we live our lives.

There was nothing wrong with the eleven other warriors choosing to go in different directions. In fact before any soul's journey through the earth plane is complete, he will have to travel through the darkness before he can truly understand the light. There are many beautiful facets and many different paths to travel on earth, but when one is ready to go all the way, the spiritual path is very simple and yet that simplicity can be very difficult. One who can follow this path directly up the mountain will be a light unto all who would follow. As Jeshua said, "I am the way the truth and the life." Jeshua became that which he was seeking and teaching. In the same way, our actions must be in alignment with our prayers if we are to make progress on our spiritual journey. Ralph Waldo Emerson summed this up very nicely in his saying: "Your actions speak so loudly, I cannot hear what you are saying."

However you pray to God, make sure that you ask that His Will be done in your life. Seeking His Will places your life in the hands of perfection in which no error or failure is possible. Suppose the captain of a ship was lost on a vast ocean with storms battering his ship on a daily basis and he had no idea which direction to take to get home. He sends out an SOS call and receives a reply from a lighthouse on the coast and is given direction on how to get home. This is exactly what this prayer does. It connects us with a spiritual beacon which will most assuredly bring us home. You may not believe it in the beginning, but if you seek God's Will in all you do your faith will continue to grow until you begin to experience the light within you which shall set you free.

Because of the prayers and efforts of many of our brothers and sisters in the past and present, a new spiritual age has dawned upon this world. For the first time in recorded history, the positive, loving consciousness and energy is more prevalent in this world than the negative. This is the beginning of a new age which will only get brighter as time goes by. I feel that this was the significance of the date, December 21, 2012. I believe that this was a demarcation point in which the positive energy in the world began to outweigh the negative. This was the first time in recorded history that this has taken place. From that point on, the positive consciousness and energy in the world began to overpower the darkness, although the darkness is not giving up control without a fight. Because of the greater light now present in the world at this time, our prayers will be more powerful and manifest more quickly than in the past.

Many who walk the spiritual path find that things seem to get more difficult in the beginning of their journey. Others encounter severe tests after they have been on the path for a while. In the story Christopher was willing to face his greatest fears because of his love and devotion to his king. He had to travel the last part of the journey all alone which each of us will have to do on our spiritual journey. No one but ourselves can really know what we are going through during this last phase. All aspirants on the spiritual journey will at one point or another encounter an initiation which is known as the 'dark night of the soul'. This is not a test that God places in front of us to see if we are worthy or not. It is we who test ourselves. It usually happens that the stronger and more dedicated the soul, the more severe the test. If we can use these difficult periods as an opportunity to let go of everything that is not real, we will be doing ourselves a great service. We are also doing a great service to all who follow after us, as we will be making the spiritual path much easier for them, just as the early pioneers made it much easier for those who followed after them. Our lives then become a manifestation of the way, the truth and the life. Our lives will then reflect the essence of what a true living prayer is.

Surrendering to the Will of God is the highest prayer a soul can make. Surrendering happens when a soul realizes that his way of doing things has only brought him pain and emptiness. As long as we are dependent on our personal will to direct our lives, we will continue to experience the darkness of this world because our personal will does not know any better. At some point we need to let go of our way of doing things and let God take over. In the bible it states that God's strength is made perfect in our weakness. What this is saying is that when we recognize that our personal will has not taken us to where we want to go and it never will, then we will naturally surrender to His Will and then our weakness will be transformed into unlimited strength.

As a person nears the end of his journey and is very close to total transformation, he will find that there is no need to question anything. The reason for this is that he will know absolutely, that God's Will and his are one and the same. Therefore, everything and I mean everything that takes place in his life is a living prayer. What need is there to question anything? One of the ego's last ditch attempts to prevent a person from breaking free is to pose questions that could bring doubt to the individual, or pose a question which has no reasonable answer such as, "How could a perfect Son of God experience such pain and darkness?" At this stage of development the aspirant simply ignores these questions with the statement, "I question nothing because I trust in God completely." The ego will try and keep us trapped in duality, but the ego is no match for the Will of God. By the way there is an answer to the ego's question which I will expound upon later in the book. There is no greater realization that a person can have before the actual transformation then to realize that her will and the Will of God are the same. When a person fully realizes this truth, through great effort on her part, she is totally free. Even though the person may not yet have fully awakened, there is an absolute assurance that the glorious event will soon take place. It's sort of like somebody in prison who has been paroled and is simply waiting for the paperwork to be completed before she can walk out of the prison gates to freedom. This state of assurance will surely come as we sincerely and persistently seek God's Will in our life.

What if a soul is not ready to fully relinquish their will to God?

There is no judgment if we are not yet ready to go all the way. We do not pick an apple from a tree when it first appears as a bud. We need to wait until it ripens and is ready to eat before picking it. In the same way, a soul whose ego is not fully developed would not be ready to relinquish their personal will. In chapter 3 of Ecclesiastes it states: 'To everything there is a season and a time to every purpose under the heaven'. The ego must be fully developed before the spiritual journey can commence in earnest. There is a greater purpose to this play of consciousness on this earth. We are explorers and creators of new consciousness which did not exist before our journey into illusion. On our spiritual journey, it is very important not to judge anyone for anything they do or do not do because we are limiting ourselves with that judgment. Each soul is creating their own experiences on this journey and each soul must face the consequences of what they are creating, whether the results are pleasant or difficult. Seek only to be a light on the path to others by living in a way that you become an example to others.

As our spiritual understanding develops, we will experience that the nature and content of our prayers will also change. People will pray to God according to their level of spiritual development. A spiritually mature prayer does not acknowledge evil or limitation as a reality. The mature prayer recognizes the true nature and oneness with God for all humanity. This prayer accepts the sacred union of all souls and gives thanksgiving to God for the sacred truth of who we are as an extension of God Himself. A mature prayer also thanks God for the awakening, because an advanced spiritual soul knows that the awakening has already taken place. One of my first spiritual teachers taught us to accept what we were striving for as an already accomplished fact. In the same way, by accepting that the awakening has already taken place, we are creating a doorway through which this truth can manifest in our lives in much less time. We must still deal with and release our current false beliefs and desires, but through the assumption that we are already the truth which we seek, we create an opening in our mind which allows us to move more rapidly in that direction.

In the gospels Jeshua said, "It is done unto you according to your faith." We can pray all we want but if we don't believe that our prayers are truly going to be answered, then we will most likely be disappointed. All the help we need is available to us if we believe. Prayer can be a tremendous tool in increasing our faith.

I will end this chapter with a funny story involving prayer that I heard many years ago. There was a preacher giving a sermon when a tremendous rain storm hit the town. The rain came down in buckets and it wasn't long before the church started to flood and the congregation left the church, but the preacher continued to preach. Soon the water was ankle deep and a man came by in a car and yelled to the preacher to get in the car but the preacher refused saying, "I'm not worried, God will take care of me", and continued to preach even though the church was empty. When the water reached knee high a man on a raft came by and yelled to the preacher to get on the raft before he drowned, but again the preacher yelled back that God would take care of him and kept on preaching. Now the water was waist high and a man came by in a power boat and pleaded with the preacher to get in the boat but the preacher again said he was not afraid, God would take care of him, so the boat left. It wasn't long before the water was neck high and a helicopter hovered over the church and a man yelled to the preacher that he better come out now or he would drown, but the preacher yelled back that God would take care of him and so the helicopter flew away. The water then got so deep that the preacher was sucked under the water and drowned. When he opened his eyes he was in heaven and immediately saw God and said, "Oh God, why didn't you save me from that horrible flood?" God replied, "I sent you a car, a raft, a power boat and a helicopter but you did not pay any attention. What else did you want me to do?"

Our sincere prayers will be answered, we just need to trust and use a little willingness and common sense.

CHAPTER 7

The Death of the I

As a deeper understanding and realization of who we are begins to settle into our consciousness, we begin to move into stage four of our spiritual journey. Stage four is when our heart consciousness begins to direct our life. This is the stage of **Becoming** in which we not only know the truth, we are the truth. At this stage we are a manifested blessing to the world because of the powerful love and light that we spread wherever we go.

It wasn't until after Little's death that I was able to enter stage four of my journey. I felt like my heart was ripped open after her departure. It was only then that I had access to the deeper facets of my heart and could allow my heart to take over as the director of my path. I experienced so many beautiful feelings and frequencies emanating from my heart during this time. My relationship with others became much more pleasant and joyous as my heart was now in charge of my life.

The problems most of us have are because of the influences and beliefs of our parents, school, media, and the people we have encountered since birth, which is a direct result of our karma or our choices. These influences have created much confusion and short circuited the information coming from our heart so that we only hear the information coming from the brain. When we reach stage four of our spiritual journey we then begin to hear and understand very clearly what our heart is saying.

In this final stage we have cleared the way for the heart to take its rightful place as the director of our lives. Our thoughts and feelings and actions are in accord with spiritual truth. It doesn't mean that we have reached a state of full spiritual development it means that the way has been cleared for us to reach this state without all the interference we were dealing with before this time. Reaching stage four doesn't mean we cannot fall back to one of the earlier stages. It really depends on our willingness to truly listen to and follow the dictates of the heart which is the same as listening to our higher self. We will probably still have a lot of issues to deal with at this stage but we will not resist them as much. We will know that absolutely everything in our life is for the purpose of service or greater self-understanding. At this point we are starting to transcend the world. We will know who we are and the purpose of our life on earth. The power of the knowing of an awakened soul has tremendous impact on the mind of the world and accelerates the transformation process of the whole world.

Stage four can be a beautiful experience but it is not the end. The final stage of growth in this particular system, would be a fully developed Christed being. It is at this stage that the individual has fully developed spiritually. This is the spiritual development which Jeshua manifested in his life as the Christ 2000 years ago. This final stage is preceded by the death of the individual self but not all who have died to the ego are at this fully developed stage.

During my spiritual journey, I have had a few spiritual insights which gave me an understanding of what it would be like at the death of my personal ego. One of the first ones happened just as I was waking up one morning about eight or nine years ago. I was shown how my final spiritual awakening was to take place. I saw myself walking across a room when all of a sudden a huge burst of brilliant white light exploded in me and the person I used to be was completely gone. In his place was a consciousness so vast, powerful and infinite, that at the time it was a little scary because of the enormous sudden change. In the years that followed, I had many beautiful and powerful spiritual experiences which gave me great insights into this amazing spiritual journey.

Another of these experiences happened on December 8, 2012. It was a very brief dream which was so powerful that I immediately woke up and could not go back to sleep. It happened about 1:30 in the morning. Even though the dream only lasted a very short time, I experienced the death of me as an individual in such a real way that it actually felt like I had died. I actually experienced what it felt like to take a quick last breath before death. It reminded me of the last breath my partner took before suddenly leaving her body. The big difference was that I was not experiencing the death of the body, but rather the annihilation of my individuality. This experience was very intense, much more so than the experience I described in the previous paragraph. After lying in bed for an hour contemplating the experience, I realized I would not be able to go back to sleep. I got dressed and went upstairs and had a cup of tea as I continued to go over the short, but powerful dream. I then turned on the computer and began writing this new chapter. These two experiences, plus a number of other ego death experiences I've had, showed me very clearly the futility of holding unto my separate identity. A soul can fulfill his spiritual purpose without the death of the ego if this is the path his soul has chosen, but there will come a lifetime when the death of our individual ego will occur.

When I was in priest class in the Holy Order of Mans, one of the exercises given to us by Father Paul was to see how long we could carry on conversations without using the word 'I'. Some of my fellow students and I would make a game of it and maybe bet a cup of coffee on who could go the longest without saying 'I'. I was surprised at how quickly I used the word I. I didn't do very well in the game. I was still very attached to my individual sense of identity.

In this day many people are having awakening experiences. There is a large awakening taking place, even amongst some who were not even interested in spirituality. Some awakenings are temporary and some are permanent. The one thing that is constant in all true awakenings, whether temporary or permanent, is that there is a realization that this world and the individuality are not real.

There are also different levels of awakening and different gifts which come with the different awakenings. In awakening, we may lose our attachment to the individuality we have identified with, but we will always have a uniqueness which is different from any other soul ever created.

My personal spiritual path has been an experience of 'death by a thousand cuts', as the saying goes. I know why I chose this very difficult path and I am totally grateful for all the help I have received along the way. The final part of my spiritual journey was like being in a boat on a river with no paddles and the boat is being carried by the current of the river. The journey on the river was not all calm and smooth as there were many rapids that I passed through along the way. I had no idea where the current was taking me, I just knew that where I was each moment was exactly where I was supposed to be. Towards the end, I did not resist anything that happened, whether pleasant or unpleasant. I enjoyed the pleasant parts of the journey and I learned from the unpleasant experiences. The unpleasant experiences were there to reveal to me certain beliefs or emotions which still needed resolution and clearing.

We are in a time of tremendous change and upheaval in the world. There is also tremendous upheaval going on within the minds and emotions of most souls on the planet at this time, including many on the spiritual path. Many are going through the dark night of the soul, which is part of the process of dying to the ego. It is said that the darkest hour is just before dawn and in this case it is literally true. Many are waking up from the illusion of this world to the great reality of who we really are. We are entering a period in which the Golden Dawn of Spiritual Awakening is taking place within individuals on a mass scale. When this world was formed and first inhabited, it was literally Paradise. We are again making it paradise as we move through this glorious process of getting in touch with the truth within us. The kingdom of heaven is within each one of us. Jeshua said that there are many beings on the other side who would love to change places with us. This earth provides an incredible opportunity for experience and spiritual growth that a soul can find nowhere else in the universe.

St. Paul said in one of his letters to the Corinthians, "I die daily." He was referring to the surrendering and dying to all the beliefs and identifications of his personal life, on a moment by moment basis so that he could be reborn into the truth of who he truly is. The journey to spiritual awakening is difficult but it is not complicated. I will use the analogy of attending a movie to reflect the awakening process. On earth when we go to a movie, each person experiences the movie with their own emotions, ideas and beliefs. Life on earth is like attending a movie. The consciousness of the individual determines how he will react or respond to the movie. Nobody in the theater is really interacting with each other, because their focus is on what is happening on the screen which we believe to be our reality. Since we believe the images on the screen are real, we get involved with the illusionary characters on the screen. Some characters we like and others we cannot stand and so we react according to the different characters that appear on the screen. There is one particular character in the movie that we completely identify with. We feel this person's pain and loss and we feel his success and happiness. We are so identified with this character in the movie that we fully believe this is who we are. We have been hypnotized by the ego into believing something which is not real. This whole movie is simply a figment of our imagination. Each character in the movie has a unique perspective of what is taking place, but just about everyone believes the world with all its pain, suffering and death is real.

Now remember, we are not interacting with the real people in the theater, because each one of them is also identified with one particular character on the screen. In fact we are not even aware that these real people exist, because we are so caught up in the illusionary movie and characters.

The illusory movie seemed to appear because of the appearance of the ego. This separated existence on earth consists of nothing but a false belief system that is taking place nowhere. As I mentioned earlier, when God created the souls, anything became possible. What appears on the screen is determined by our beliefs, desires and will. None of the screen characters are real. They are simply part of our dream scenario. We and we alone determine what our experience on the screen is going to be. As our spiritual understanding develops, we take greater control over what appears on the screen of our mind. At some point in our individual movie we enter the dying process of our own personal ego and this is where our personal illusory movie ends, very happily I must say.

Escaping from the illusion of this world can be likened to a person in the theater getting out of his chair, turning his back on the screen of illusion and walking out into the bright sunlight of reality. In order to do this, he must give up his identification with everything on the screen of unreality. This is the death of the ego. When a person leaves the theater of illusion, he will see life as it truly is in all its glory, love, joy, peace and beauty. After his awakening, he can walk back into the theater, bringing the light of wisdom with him because he has realized who he is and can then help others to also leave the theater of illusion and death. As we leave the theater of illusion we experience the pure joy and unity of all life

As long as we are caught up in illusion, it may seem like the process of awakening takes a long time. It all depends on our willingness to know truth and our willingness to deny illusion. There is so much spiritual light entering the earth right now that the process of awakening has really taken on an accelerated pace for those who are ready for the truth. We just have to be willing to let go of the illusions and beliefs that keep us in the dark.

Be patient and persistent. Patience was one of the most difficult lessons I had to learn. I was like the majority of people who always wanted things to happen immediately. This is an attitude which is very prevalent in America and spreading around the world. Look at all the fast food restaurants, drive through cleaners and a myriad of other institutions which provide instant gratification to the masses. The path to awakening is a process in the mind that does seem to take some time, but the final result is absolutely assured.

In the 1960's, Timothy Leary, the LSD guru, had a saying: "Turn on, tune in and drop out." He was trying to get people to open their eyes to all the greed, corruption and hypocrisy of those in power. By recommending that people take LSD, he was hoping that they would see that our society was trying to give us a blue print on how our lives should be lived in order to be successful. His message was that the success the world was preaching simply led to emptiness, disillusionment and finally death. Mr. Leary was on the right track but his methods could only take a person so far and unfortunately many who traveled that path wound up very dysfunctional.

We have never done anything wrong. If we can fully accept this truth, we won't be afraid to meet God face to face. Think of the one person you love more than anybody in the whole world. Now imagine that you have been separated from this person for ten years. Imagine how happy you would be to be reunited with this person. Our reunification with God will be experienced with unimaginable joy. Many of us may feel that we are not pure enough to meet with God because of what the world has programmed us to believe about ourselves. Underneath all the false concepts, judgments and beliefs we have about ourselves, each one of us is totally pure and holy. We not only deserve to meet with God, each one of us is a unique part of God. We are God walking upon the earth, so how much more deserving are we of everything that is.

Don't be afraid when the ego starts to go through its death throes. This is not your death, but rather your rebirth into the Glory of God. It is only an illusion which dies. I mentioned several times before that once the ego becomes aware of your efforts to free yourself from its clutches, it will get very upset and try everything to stop you from seeing the truth. Remember this when you are going through difficult times. Observe what is happening in you without judging it in any way. Difficult times are opportunities to learn more about ourselves and the ego.

One thing I still don't understand is that you speak of the ego as a thing that does exists and on the other hand you say it does not exist. How can it be both ways?

In this world of illusion the ego does exist, because we believe it does. You must understand that even though this world does not exist in reality, it does exist in the mind of people who are caught up in illusion. Because we are children of God, our beliefs have great power regardless of whether the belief is based on illusion or reality. Jeshua said, "Be it unto you as you believe." Illusion does not affect God, but it unfortunately seems to have an effect on the believer. As long as we believe in duality of any kind, the ego will exist in our mind. At some point in creation all darkness will disappear from our minds as if it had never been there.

One of the final lessons on my journey to Self-Realization had to do with the need of fully integrating my inner child. As I mentioned in chapter one, I had a very difficult childhood. As a result, there was a part of me that disassociated itself from the whole. Not only did I have to heal the inner child from this life time, but I had to heal the deepest wound of my soul which was the seeming separation from our Mother/Father God. This is the deepest of all pains that each of us will eventually have to face before we are able to return home for good. The true spiritual path is a glorious and amazing journey and I send my love and blessings to all who are on this glorious path of Self Realization.

In conclusion to this chapter, I just want to remind you one more time that all the forces in heaven and earth are at your beckon call once you truly make up your mind to return to God. There are many who are in a physical body at this time that God has sent to help the masses of people in this time of great opportunity. Don't be deceived by all the darkness that is prevalent in the world today. Many things will happen in the next few years which will be very frightening to the masses. We have just completed a 26,000 year cycle which culminated on December 21st, 2012. At the end of a cycle there are always old things that need to be discarded to make way for the new. This process is now taking place on many levels. The energies and opportunities to awaken are now more available to us than at any other time because of the age we live in.

The TV series **The X-files**, always ended with the saying, **"The truth is out there."** Well, the truth is within each of us and is totally available to anyone who has the courage to seek it. The happiness which we all crave is at hand. I only pray that the hearts and minds of all mankind will be open to receive of this grace. God bless you all with His perfect Love, Light and Strength as you walk the holy path back unto Him. I speak to you as a humble brother and servant.

CHAPTER 8

True Forgiveness

One of the most difficult lessons for me to embody on my spiritual journey was self-forgiveness. I was always my harshest critic and felt like I had to be perfect or I was a failure. Perfection in the realm of duality is an illusion and so I was trying to live up to an impossible concept of what I thought I needed to be. I can remember that as far back as a child of three I was striving for a state of perfection. Little did I know that this striving to be perfect was actually a barrier to reaching the state of freedom and oneness that I so longed for. During the first 30 years of my spiritual journey in this life, I crucified myself internally whenever I made mistakes. This attitude created intense stress in my body and a severe restriction and fear in my ability to fully relate with others.

At one point, the fear and tension that I experienced when relating to groups caused a real problem in my life and I was intent of finding out the cause. The only thing I knew for sure was that this fear began a very short time after joining the Holy Order of Mans. I wanted so badly to find out the cause of this fear and tension that I made an appointment to see a hypnotherapist. I was thinking that the cause came from the traumas that filled my childhood. The hypnotherapist induced a state of deep relaxation in me and told me to get in touch with the fear and tension and to use that as a vehicle to go back to the initial cause of this state of unease. I very clearly saw myself going back in time to being a child and then into another lifetime and saw myself in a tunic and sandals. I saw that I was a spiritual leader in that life and had a large following. The people in power at that time were only seeking more power and were not doing the people's will so at one point I encouraged my followers to overthrow the existing establishment and many died in the process of the rebellion. I was then put in power. By this time I was so remorseful and critical of myself for what I felt was an abuse of my position as a spiritual guide that I withdrew from public life and faded into the background. I lived the final years of that life in a state of deep seclusion and remorse. I then saw a number of lives that immediately followed this lifetime and in each one, I was a monk who lived a very austere and penitent life. I literally crucified myself for having made this mistake as a spiritual leader. I now understood why I felt I had to be perfect and was so critical of myself in this life for any mistake I made as I did not want to repeat the mistakes of the past. Reading the section on forgiveness in The Disappearance of the Universe really helped me in the process of releasing the guilt I had carried inside me for so long.

If there are only a few ideas in this book that a person fully understands and consistently uses in their daily life, then I hope one of them is forgiveness. True forgiveness is our key to liberation.

Can a person reach the state of awakening without forgiveness?

Forgiveness allows us to experience our innocence. Innocence is realized through dissolving the guilt and darkness in our mind. Forgiveness allows us to experience that our innocence was never lost which opens the door to our awakening. A person must somehow be freed of all the accumulated guilt and false beliefs in order to awaken. Having spiritual experiences is not the end of the story, although these experiences will open us up to more light. Forgiving ourselves is the simplest and easiest way to allow the light into our minds. Realizing that we were only dreaming makes it a lot easier to release our guilt.

You said that we must let go of all negativity in our minds. How are we able to do that when we have no idea how much negativity we have, or what it is? How do we know what kind of karma we have accumulated?

The way we want to approach forgiveness is to forgive our self and others for anything we are conscious of. We don't need to worry about our unconscious guilt. If there is a need for the unconscious guilt in us to be brought to our conscious awareness, it will happen at the perfect time. The Holy Spirit will help us in releasing the guilt we are unaware of, as long as we forgive what we are aware of. We must do our part and be vigilant in forgiving everything in our life of which we are conscious. We should practice forgiving our self and others for every negative thought, feeling and action. This includes those little irritations and impatience. We should forgive our self for any pain or sickness we experience because those symptoms are a manifestation of some guilt or fear in our mind. In my spiritual journey, I forgave myself for anything that created discomfort in my life, including something like a slight headache. If I had a headache I would say or think something like this to myself: "I forgive myself completely for whatever guilt or false belief there is in my mind which caused the headache. Yet as I forgive myself for whatever the seeming cause is, I know that I am forgiving myself for an illusion, for a bad dream I am having and I forgive the dreamer of this dream." You can shorten your statement of forgiveness or substitute anything for headache and it will work. Change the wording as you like but always remain faithful to the premise of true forgiveness. We all have plenty to do in forgiving ourselves for things we are conscious of and we can be assured that the Holy Spirit will help us with the rest. It is extremely important to remember that we are forgiving ourselves or others for something that never really happened. Forgive, forgive and then forgive some more.

A Course in Miracles states that the physical universe and everything in it is illusion. It also states that the only illusion we can use to help free us from this dream state is **forgiveness**. Forgiveness is an illusion because in reality we have nothing to forgive. The keys to the Kingdom of Heaven are contained in the understanding of what forgiveness really means. I hope that after reading this chapter you will have that understanding. The forgiveness that many religions practice is based on a good principal, but it won't set us free because it is based on the belief that a person has committed sins and is guilty. This type of forgiveness supports the belief that sin is real. We all make mistakes in our worldly journey but as we develop spiritually it is our responsibility to learn from those mistakes. Mistakes can be corrected, but letting go of the illusion of sin is more difficult. True forgiveness is based on the understanding that we are forgiving images in our mind which have no real existence. We are forgiving ourselves and others for a false belief, a bad dream and nothing more.

When we sincerely start to walk the spiritual path, the ego will be very quick to judge and condemn us for any little thing that we appear to do wrong. If we are not vigilant about the ego's underhanded tactics, we will find ourselves believing the ego and thus join it in judging and condemning ourselves and others. Judging and condemning ourselves is a pit fall that just about all of us on the path fall into many, many times. We think we are being righteous by condemning ourselves for any wrongs we think we have done. This is one of the main tricks the ego uses to keep us from the truth. It is extremely important not to let ourselves fall into the trap of self-condemnation.

There is a facet of the ego which is very important for us to understand if we are going to begin using true forgiveness. The ego encourages us to project our guilt onto others. This act of projection does not relieve us of our guilt, but it does seem to bring relief for a short while. In the long run it is simply creating another event we will have to forgive. Projection comes in many forms, but it is always for the purpose of relieving ourselves of our inner guilt. The ego has programmed us to be mortally afraid of looking at our inner guilt in order to ensure its' continued existence. The ego is afraid that if we looked deeply within ourselves, we would discover that we really have nothing to be guilty about. A very cruel hoax has been played on us and we have bought into this lie. We then seek to avoid the pain and anxiety that comes from the feeling of guilt in us by projecting it unto others. The majority of the world practices projection in one form or another.

How many countless times when we are feeling bad do we find some exterior person or situation to blame for our problems? If we take a close look at the next time we blame or condemn someone else, we will find that we feel a little bit better or self-righteous for the time being. We may actually feel downright good. The reason for this is that we seem to be projecting some of our inner guilt unto some other person place or thing in order to relieve some of that pressure inside ourselves. The problem is that there is no other person, place or thing. This is our dream and our dream only. Everybody and everything in our dream is a part of ourselves and that is why it is so important to forgive others, because by forgiving others we are literally forgiving ourselves. It's interesting that psychiatrists and psychologists will tell us that all the people in our dreams are an aspect of our own personality. It's the same thing with our everyday waking dream. Everything is happening in our mind. So we can project as much as we want, but this will not lessen our pain because the pain will still remain within us. We are simply projecting it unto another image in our mind which we will eventually have to face.

Forgiveness is a soothing balm which will begin the process of true healing in our mind. We need to start forgiving ourselves instead of projecting our guilt unto others. Becoming aware of our guilt and having the courage to face it, without judging or condemning ourselves or others is the key to releasing it.

The projection of guilt is very clearly played out in our political system. It seems that the politician who does a better job in blaming their opponent is usually the one who gets elected. The two party political system is an ideal situation in which the ego can use the tool of projection to create animosity and separation between people. The projection game is also frequently played out in the parent and child relationship where the child will blame the parent for his situation in life. Another relationship where this projection seems to take place quite often is through the partner relationship. When we become aware of our projecting unto others in whatever situation it occurs, we are taking a big step towards enlightenment.

To blame another for our condition in life, is like Joe blaming the delivery boy for delivering the ice cream Joe himself ordered. Joe knew before he ordered it that he was allergic to dairy and yet he still insisted on ordering it and then blaming somebody else for his allergic reaction. So the delivery boy became his scapegoat.

One of the most difficult ego traps is the act of comparing ourselves to others. We all have the tendency to compare ourselves with others. The whole word revolves around competition and being better than our neighbors. This is the nature of duality. The cure for the disease of comparison and competition is the realization that we are all one. Only when we can look through the eyes of oneness can we see each other as we truly are. An enlightened mind sees no difference or separation between his self and others. Spiritual knowledge opens the door to pure love which reveals the oneness of all things.

If we were to have access to the moment by moment thoughts of the great majority of people, we would become aware that almost one hundred per cent of their thoughts are ego directed. Just about all thoughts in this world are based on the assumption that we are individuals and separate from everybody else. How willing are we to let go of the idea of individuality? Our truthful answer will reveal how ready we are to pursue the truth that will set us free.

It is not an easy task to dissolve the voice of the ego, but it can be and must be done if we are to fully awaken spiritually. We must become spiritual warriors to break free of the illusionary ropes that the ego uses to keep us bound. This requires letting go of some of our exterior activities in order to create a space for some quiet time. We will grow rapidly in our spiritual pursuit by learning to sit still and quiet our minds. Our determination can transcend any difficulties the ego places in front of us. We are children of God and are as powerful as we can accept. It is extremely important to constantly be aware of the voice within us and to be able to determine whether it is coming from the Holy Spirit or the ego. We are so used to accepting the dictates of the ego as our own voice, that it becomes very easy to think we are listening to the Holy Spirit, when in fact it is the voice of the ego we are hearing. When you are in a situation and not sure how to act, ask yourself how love would respond to the situation. Eventually we will open up to enough light that there will be no question on how to respond. Remember that the ego will do everything in its power to prevent us from reaching this state of realization.

Let's look at some other examples of how projection manifests in our lives, because just about everybody does it. We read about criminals and see them as evil. We see other nations who do not believe the way we do and say they are wrong. We have personal enemies whom we hate and curse. We get in a fight with our wife or husband and blame them for us not being happy. We buy a car and find out later it is a lemon and curse the sales person. We get in a car accident and blame the person driving the other car. We have an operation and it does not turn out well and we sue the doctor. We're late for work and we blame the traffic. All these and many other blame games are forms of projecting our discomfort unto others. These projections appear in many forms, but it is all based on our lack of knowing the truth. In order to get away from the pain or unease we feel, we project the blame unto others so that we can feel better about ourselves. Many times, we are the target of our own projection of guilt when something bad happens, but this is no different than blaming others. It serves the same purpose of perpetuating guilt and reinforcing the idea of guilt.

It sounds like you're saying that nobody is guilty and we should just let things happen as they may.

It is true that nobody is guilty of anything because everything that we experience is happening in our own mind. There is really nobody else out there. We are the creator and the witness of everything that happens in our life. The power is in our hands and we can choose to change what seems to appear in our lives, or we can go on blindly believing that we are victims of the world. It is the consciousness and understanding with which we do something that determines whether we are perpetuating or dissolving the mental chains that bind us to this world. As long as our false beliefs keep this world going, our world will operate on the belief of good and evil, because the very nature of this world is duality. The only thing that will ever change our perception of the world is by forgiving ourselves and waking up. True lasting change comes when a person accepts the truth that she and she alone has created, or chosen, everything she is experiencing. That is the one real positive thing that can be taught in this world. A Course in Miracles states that we should not seek to change the world, but rather change our perception of the world. The only true change or transformation takes place in our mind.

What we believe about ourselves and the world becomes the essence of who we become as a person and determines what we experience. Our false beliefs distort everything we think and see. We see through a glass darkly as stated by St. Paul in one of his letters to the Corinthians. Forgiveness reveals our true sight and allows us to see clearly. Remember, everybody's experiences are different and so the way each person sees an event would also be slightly different. This has been proven by questioning several people about an event they all experienced. If there were twelve people who saw an event, whether an accident or something else, you will most likely get twelve slightly different interpretations. If we have all these differences in our perceptions of what we see in the outer world, then shouldn't we question what reality is since there are so many different personal versions of it?

Then what is real?

Reality will be revealed to us as our spiritual light grows bright enough and allows us to see life as it really is. We need physical light to see in the physical world just as we need spiritual light to see spiritual reality. Reality cannot be taught to someone who does not want to know, just as spiritual truths cannot be understood by the intellectual mind. To try and grasp reality with the intellect is like putting an encyclopedia in front of a mouse and expecting it to understand it. Let me answer your question in another way. Reality is God and each one of us is a unique part of God. The essence of truth lies in the understanding that we are one with God. Our oneness with God has nothing to do with our bodies, our individuality or this world. This is who we are but our ego does not want us to realize this truth. Light is the darkness most feared by the ego. Spiritual light dissolves the illusion of the ego. When a person is truly ready to let go of their ego, forgiveness will accelerate their process to awakening.

Forgiveness begins a process of removing the layers of film which have covered our true sight. The more layers we remove through our forgiveness efforts, the more light is available to us. The more light we have, the more we remember and experience who we really are. We are aware that without light we cannot see what is happening in this physical world and yet even on the brightest of days, what we see with our physical eyes has nothing to do with reality. Our vision and perspective is completely distorted because our physical eyes only relay to our brain, pictures, sounds, and feelings of an illusionary world. Spiritual light is very different from ordinary light. To see with spiritual vision is to realize the truth behind the veil of illusion. The physical eyes see through the eyes of separation and comparison, whereas spiritual vision sees the oneness and perfection in all that is.

A fully awakened individual may appear to be in the world, but is in no way attached to it. This may shed some light on the statement made by Jeshua, "I am in the world, but not of it." Jeshua knew that the world was not real, just a dream, but he seemed to function in it because this was his way of helping us to awaken from the dream.

If what you are saying is true, why does it appear that we are all having the same dream? We all get similar information about world events.

This is because we all have an agreement to experience the world in the way we do. We might call this a contract of the mass consciousness of the world and of each soul entering this dimension. We needed this agreement between each other to have some semblance of order in experiencing a dimension of duality with linear time and space. We experience this earth with the belief that we are separated so that we can each create our own reality from different perspectives. Therefore we all share in a similar dream using our unique perspective to experience and choose what our soul wants to experience. This determines what type of dream experience we will have. As I mentioned before, when an audience experiences a movie there will be many different feelings and perspectives about the movie, because of the different beliefs and emotional states within each of us. It's the same movie and yet there will be many different reactions to the different characters and scenes. We all seem to be looking at the same world, but our perspectives and interpretations depend on our state of consciousness. Just think what we could do if we all chose to see the world as a place of love and joy. What an amazing transformation of the world this would create in a very short time.

Our will is the determining factor as to when we will choose to awaken from this dream. It is very important to remember that the dream is not taking place in the world or in a body. It is taking place in our mind and it is in our mind where the choice and changes have to be made. When we make the choice to change, we activate the heart center which is where God dwells within each of us. We must understand that the world of perception is a world of effects. The cause is in the mind. What we believe is true, is true for us and that determines what we seem to experience. To follow the path of awakening we must go through a process of expanding our consciousness and forgiveness accelerates this process.

If none of this really happened, then why do we need to forgive anybody?

<u>Because we believe it really happened</u>. We are really forgiving our own false beliefs, our individual dream and this is why we need to begin with self-forgiveness. Let me give you an idea of what it is you are forgiving yourself for. Suppose you just watched a movie about a bank robbery on TV. After the movie you are sitting on your couch and for a moment you let your mind wander and think of yourself as being a bank robber and killing one of the guards as you make your get away. You then snap out of it thinking what a silly idea that was and get on with your day. Do you think you should be sent to jail for this fleeting thought? Life on earth is a dream and most of us have not forgiven ourselves for the dream we are having. Many souls, as of this date, are not yet ready to give up the dream of illusion and that is perfectly fine. We can continue in this sleep state as long as we desire. There is no condemnation or judgment if that is our choice.

How could a thought like this arise in the Mind of God if He is perfect? How could He allow us to experience such pain and tragedy? How can we help people who are suffering if we believe none of this is actually happening?

We all have free will and we are all unique and with that combination anything is possible. Also, when you realize the profound positive impact on all creation that our journey into illusion is having, you will understand the divine purpose of this journey. I will address this purpose more fully in a later chapter. Let me answer your question in this way. I will again use the analogy of watching a movie. This time I will liken us to the projectionist in the booth upstairs. Our mind is symbolic of a projectionist who projects his beliefs, desires and fears on the screen of life. There are billions of projectionists and each one is projecting their own character on the screen. There is an agreement between all the projectionists to share in the same movie from their own personal perspective. Each projectionist believes that the movie on the screen is really happening. Now suppose one of the projectionists wakes up and sees that the movie is just and illusion and is not really real. Through his awakened state, his character on the screen starts emanating a great deal of light which begins affecting many of the other projectionists and many of them also start to awaken. This is how an enlightened being can affect so many without saying a word.

Have you ever been asleep and had somebody shine a bright light in your face? Unless we were in a very, very deep sleep, the light would awaken us. A spiritually awaken person will naturally allow his light to shine upon the world so that others may awaken. We are not seeking to awaken the character in the movie, but the projectionist in the booth. It is the dreamer of the movie who needs to be awakened and not the dream character on the screen. Does this give you a better idea of how we can help others and still not give credence to this illusion?

As long as we operate from the assumption that we are the character on the screen, we will not be able to help others or ourselves. The intellect will never be able to accept a satisfactory answer to your questions, because the intellect is a function of the ego. When a person reaches a certain degree of spiritual awakening, he will realize that his individuality, the world and the entire physical universe in which we seem to live never had any real existence. His belief in separation will completely disappear from his mind. He will know absolutely that none of this ever happened. This truth must be experienced to truly understand it.

A spiritually awake person does not deny that others are going through a lot of suffering because she has been through her share of suffering. She understands that if she is to help others she must have the realization that suffering cannot exist in God and therefore it cannot be real. Our realization that it is not real is the only way we can truly help others. In quantum physics it has been discovered that there is nothing in this world that is real unless we observe it. It is our belief that seems to make things real in the illusionary realm of time. Outside of illusion, there is only one truth and that is God. If we focus on the suffering of ourselves and others as real, we are giving life and power to those conditions and circumstances and thus we make it real in our life. We should have compassion for others and not pity. Pity validates the illusion. If we become a conscious observer of illusion, then that which is not real will eventually disappear and we'll be able to see clearly so that we can help those who are ready to receive it.

If we truly want to help others and ourselves, then we will do whatever is necessary to free ourselves from the illusion of the ego so that we become a great source of light to all who seek the light. Jeshua said, "Greater love has no man than this, that he lay down his life for his friends." What this statement does not reveal is that the life we are laying down is the illusionary life which is causing us all our pain and depression. So as we forgive ourselves and surrender our personal ego, we are actually performing the greatest act of love for ourselves as well as for others.

Please don't think you are being uncaring of others by inwardly refusing to give credence to their pain. If Jeshua had believed that the affliction in the person he was healing was real, he would not have been able to heal them. He saw the perfection in each person he was healing. True compassion is doing what is necessary to help others to free themselves from their guilt, which is the cause of pain. An awakened being will have compassion for others because he understands what they seem to be going through. He traveled the same roads that others seem to be traveling. At the same time he doesn't exacerbate the situation by believing that the suffering of others is real. Don't give life to whatever is causing you pain, but rather focus on that which will free you from the illusion which seems to be causing the pain. Of course we should never be insensitive to others by telling them that their suffering is not real

When we practice forgiveness of ourselves or others, it would be a good idea to ask the help of the Holy Spirit, because only He knows the full implication of everything involved in the forgiveness process. We only see the surface appearances of what seems to be happening in the world. We are not aware of all the previous causes which brought the event into manifestation. Judging an event solely on the current circumstances is like looking at an iceberg and thinking that what we see is all there is to the iceberg. The great majority of the iceberg is hidden under water. In the same way, we have no way of knowing all the possible causes which have brought about the current event we are observing. The Holy Spirit is aware of the thoughts, feelings and intentions of the individual committing the act. He is aware of all the past causes of this act and the present and future implications of the act. Remember the Holy Spirit does not forgive the act itself, but rather a wrong state of mind, a false belief.

A Course in Miracles states that the ego cannot exist without judgment. Don't make the mistake of missing the incredible depth and importance of this statement. In this world, judgment is as natural as breathing. Whenever we see somebody we know very well, we see that person with all sorts of preconceived opinions as to who they are. All the experiences we have had with them colors the way we perceive them. All these beliefs and feelings about the person perpetuate an illusionary image of that person in our mind. We may not look at this as judgment, but when a certain state of spiritual awareness is realized, our perceptions of others will change completely. The belief system of this world is the antithesis of the truth. That is why spiritual aspirants have to question whether their belief system is helping them to awaken, or keeping them sound asleep. When a soul has laid aside all judgments, he is very near the door of full awakening.

I don't know how anyone could be expected not to have preconceived beliefs about people they know very well. Our perception of this world is made up from everything we have experienced in life, including our relationships and beliefs about others.

Your statement underlines the importance of striving to completely reverse the way we see the world. Seeing others you have known for years in a totally new way may sound difficult, but let me give you an analogy which will help in this process. Imagine that a kindergarten class was putting on a show for Halloween. In the show, each child had a cardboard cutout of different ghouls and other scary images which they carried in front of them as they spoke their part. Everybody in the audience knew that behind the scary cutout was an innocent child. The audience would probably think the play was cute and would not be afraid of the cutouts.

People carry many, many different personas that they project out into the world. A person might project the identity of a lawyer, a housewife, a thief, a homeless person and many other projections. All of these images carry as much reality as the cutouts that the children carried in their Halloween play. These images have nothing to do with the soul that is behind these images. The image is only a temporary mask that the soul has put on. To see past these illusory images is to begin seeing with spiritual sight. Through willingness and diligence a person will soon perceive the world with an entirely new awareness.

If we are heavily invested in the ego, then forgiving ourselves and others will be very difficult, because the ego's life blood comes through judgment of ourselves and others. Over and over again we make decisions as to whether we choose to remain separated by choosing judgment, or seek to return to a state of unity by choosing forgiveness. The choice is ours and ours alone. The relinquishment of judgment means that we are no longer able to project our guilt onto anybody or anything. Be aware of how judgments are so much a part of our so called normal thought process. This should give us an understanding of why A Course in Miracles says that we must transform our mind by having a complete reversal of our belief system in order to wake up. The thought process of the ego is insane, so our choice is between insanity or sanity. Try to envision another person not as physical body, but rather as a divine spirit, a child of God. This process will takes practice and time, but as I stated before, the spiritual journey is beyond question the greatest and highest quest a person could possibly pursue. We can use time to continue the cycle of birth and death, or we can use time to wake up from this dream. It all depends on how we use our mind and our will while we are in a body.

If we practice seeing everything that happens in our life without judgment or resistance, we are well on our way to a new life. I will share a fictional story I heard many years ago which I hope will inspire you to accept whatever happens in your life without resistance: Once there was a monk who lived in a small town in Japan. One of the unmarried women of the town became pregnant and the people of the town demanded to know who the father was. The woman wanted to protect her lover, so she told the people that the monk was the father. The people ran to the monk's hut and started yelling and cursing him. The monk did not deny the story and remaining very peaceful looked at the people and said, "Ah so." Several months later when the woman had given birth to the child, the people of the town took the baby away from her and took it to the monk who they felt had the responsibility of raising the child. When the people saw the monk they again cursed him for his evil deed and handed him the baby. He gently received the baby, looked at the people and said, "Ah so." After a couple of weeks the mother of the baby could not bear to be without her child, so she told the people the truth about who the real lover was and that the couple planned on getting married. The people ran to the monk's hut and retrieved the baby and profusely apologized to the monk for their false accusations. The monk looked at them and simply replied, "Ah so."

It is difficult for most of us to refrain from judging somebody we don't like, even if they have not done anything to us personally. It is almost impossible for most of us not to project judgment on somebody when they have said or done something mean against us, with or without justification. The monk in the story represented somebody who knew perfectly well that nobody could hurt or judge him except himself. He didn't need to justify himself to an illusion. He accepted everything that happened to him with total peace because he knew who he was. Wouldn't it be great if we could all experience that state of equanimity all the time? Well we can, and we will if we are persistent in our endeavor to wake up from this dream we are having.

Forgiveness is the opposite of judgment. Judgment binds us to the very idea or situation which we are judging. True forgiveness slowly dissolves our attachment to illusion. Forgiveness sounds like it should be an easy thing to do, but anyone who has really been hurt by someone knows that forgiving somebody and really meaning it are very different. Webster's Dictionary defines forgiveness as: excusing for a fault or offense; renouncing anger or resentment against; to absolve from payment. These definitions are fine for our worldly understanding, but do not describe what true forgiveness is. Each of the dictionary definitions, imply that a person is absolving another for some misdeed or fault. This type of forgiveness gives reality to the idea that somebody did something harmful for which they should be forgiven. It puts the cause outside of us and not where it should be, which is within our own mind.

A great practice is seeing the purity, innocence, perfection and divinity in others and our self. This is a very powerful exercise in freeing ourselves from the hell of the ego. It slowly opens up a new way of seeing which is not related to our physical eyes, but instead this practice strengthens our spiritual vision and supports our understanding of truth.

It is only our false mental concepts and beliefs that need to be forgiven. When you come right down to it, the only thing we ever have to forgive ourselves for is our belief that we are separate from God. As we practice forgiving ourselves we naturally begin to forgive the belief that we are separate from God and each other. We never sinned or offended God in anyway and in fact, as I have stated before, we have actually added to God's creation by taking the plunge into illusion.

We are the only one capable of forgiving ourselves. Even a very highly developed spiritual being cannot forgive us if we refuse to accept it. It is said that Jeshua could not perform great miracles for the people in the town where he grew up, because the people could not accept that this person, who grew up in their midst, could be such a great being. When Jeshua healed others, he told them that it was their faith which allowed him to heal them. It was their belief which allowed the energy to flow for the healing to take place. If they were not open to the healing, it could not be done. In electricity there is a need to have both a positive and negative polarity in order for energy to flow. To receive a healing, either from another or ourselves, we must be open to the fact that we are deserving of a healing. We must be receptive to the fact that in the core of our being, we are perfect and always have been.

Healing is synonymous with forgiveness. You cannot have true healing without forgiveness. We've all heard the saying, "As you forgive, so shall you be forgiven." Sounds like a nice cliché doesn't it? If we would really make the effort to put these words into practice, we would unleash a force so powerful, that it would literally transform our life in a very short time. There would be no need for hospitals and doctors if the people of the world would learn to truly forgive themselves. True forgiveness will eventually dissolve the whole physical universe and forgiveness will become obsolete. In the realm of time, this is still a long, long ways away. In our current sleep state forgiveness contains the key to everything we could ever possibly want and more. Our understanding that this world is an illusion and that we have never done anything wrong is the beginning of permanent healing.

The makers of the movie 'The Matrix' did a great job in portraying the illusion of the world. We live in a dream world, and yet this dream world is governed by a law of cause and effect. The law of cause and effect does not determine what is good or bad. The universal law of cause and effect operates on the principal that whatever we create mentally, emotionally and physically is what we must experience. A fully awakened individual invokes the law of cause and effect in a very powerful and positive way. Unfortunately in this world the majority of people invoke the law of cause and effect in a way which keeps them caught up in illusion. Wars and everything else in this world are simply a reflection of thoughts and beliefs by individuals, cities, countries, and the whole world. If we forgive the world, we become free from all the pain and darkness in the world.

Remember we are all creators and our every though is a creation in itself. We will eventually experience the effects of our negative thought patterns if they are not forgiven or changed. It is important to know that there is no right or wrong in the world, it is only our judgmental minds which make it so. Shakespeare had the right idea in one of his plays in which Hamlet says, "There is nothing good or bad, but thinking makes it so."

What about a baby who is in a war zone, who has not had a chance to think these horrible thoughts, why should they be subjected to these cruelties?

We must remember that we have had many dream cycles with many different bodies. This is what the metaphysical people would refer to as reincarnation. I prefer to use the term dream cycles because it more fully reflects the unreality of our different lifetimes. The dream cycles continue until the spirit awakens. A baby born into a difficult situation is simply experiencing a belief system she carried from previous dream cycles, or the soul may have chosen that experience for a specific reason. Just because we leave our body at death does not mean we leave all our beliefs, desires and karma with it. We may not be able to take our money with us when we die, but our karma continues on with us until we have had a chance to neutralize it through our actions and forgiveness. When a child in school fails all their classes in a certain grade, he must return to the same grade after his summer vacation in order to learn the lessons he failed to learn the year before. Life here on earth is like a school and we keep returning until we have mastered all its lessons.

Are you saying that no matter what somebody has done, that all they have to do is forgive themselves and they will be free?

Unfortunately, letting go of our guilt is a process. It is a process of slowly but surely releasing layer after layer of guilt, fears and false beliefs. In other words, it is a process of letting go of our identification with the ego. True forgiveness eventually allows a person to realize he has never done anything wrong, that he was simply hypnotized into believing in a world of illusion. Reversing these beliefs will take some time and patience. The important thing is to apply our understanding of the truth in each moment and leave the final release up to God.

I am still unclear about something. You said nobody exists in the world and yet you say we should help others, isn't this a contradiction?

If you had a child who was having a bad dream and was yelling and kicking the blankets, wouldn't you want to wake the child up and tell her it was just a bad dream? Waking her up does not mean that you are giving credence to the dream. A spiritual person is not helping somebody in the world, she is helping the soul awaken from the world. Do you see the difference between the two? A person who has awakened from the dream while in a body can be of tremendous assistance in helping others to also awaken. A person who has spiritual insights, but has still not fully awakened, can also be of great help to others. In helping others to understand the unreal nature of the world, he is helping himself to move closer to the full awakening. Helping others is the same as helping ourselves, because it is our dream and everybody in our dream represents a part of our self. We are really helping our self to awaken from a dream.

What if I don't want to wake up from this dream? Maybe I like it here. Is that wrong?

No, of course not, you have the free will to continue in the cycle of birth and death as long as you desire. There is absolutely no judgment or condemnation of a person if he chooses to remain in the world for as long as he desires. In fact young souls have to reach a certain stage of ego development before they should even consider a spiritual path. They need the experience of both the dark and the light before they are ready to enter the path of Christ Consciousness.

There is no such thing as right or wrong. There is no time limit to the dream of illusion. Each one of us is creating our own individual path in life and each one of us will have to make our own choices as to when we want to wake up. Remember, God does not judge, we make all decisions and judgments regarding our individual soul journey. Once we fully realize this truth, we are in total control of our destiny.

Here's a metaphor on the process of forgiveness. One day a traveler from a distant planet visited another world in which he found all the inhabitants to be insane. The traveler found it very puzzling that the people in this strange world acted in a way that was totally contradictory to their own happiness and peace. He wondered why these people loved pain and suffering so much. He then discovered that the water and food which the people of this world were drinking and eating had been contaminated with a virus which caused insanity. Being a very wise and spiritual being, the traveler knew exactly what to do to cure their insanity. He went to work and created an anti-virus potion to cure insanity. The potion he concocted was imbued with the vibrations and frequencies needed to counteract the virus. He then put this potion into the drinking water. After drinking the water for some time, the people of this strange world all seemed to come to the same realization. They realized that their insane thoughts, words and actions, while under the influence of the virus, were bringing about the opposite conditions from what they really wanted to experience. This realization caused them to laugh long and hard at their former beliefs. This realization freed them all and they departed with the traveler to a world of great love, joy and peace. True forgiveness is the anti-virus to the insanity of the false ego but remember we and we alone are the only one who can make that decision to forgive.

Why do you keep using the word guilt when speaking about forgiveness?

Guilt is the result of beliefs that we have done things which have offended God and deserve to be punished. Forgiveness dissolves this false belief and thus dissolves the guilt.

To conclude this all important chapter on true forgiveness, I will very briefly explain the paradox of forgiveness. True forgiveness is the ultimate key in freeing ourselves from our own delusion, so it is immensely important that we understand the nature of forgiveness. We are forgiving ourselves and everyone else for something that we or they never did. We are forgiving ourselves and all others for things done in a place that never existed. We are forgiving ourselves and others so that we can be freed from an unreality which never existed. We are forgiving ourselves and others for nothing, in order to remember and inherit everything which is our birthright. The only thing we ever have to forgive ourselves and others for, is the false belief that we are guilty. This is the paradox and the power of true forgiveness.

We should ponder that last paragraph very deeply because it is of paramount importance that we understand it completely. Understanding true forgiveness is our key to our spiritual awakening.

Faith

What is faith? St. Thomas Aquinas said: "Faith is a habit of the mind whereby eternal life is begun in us making the intellect assent to what is non-apparent." Thomas Aquinas uses the word habit to depict a way of thinking and acting that is so automatic that it becomes a part of us. We all come in with different degrees of faith depending on our soul development and how we have used our free will in past dream cycles. Just like an athlete becomes great in his field as a result of a lot of hard work, so does a soul gain spiritual faith the more he uses his will to surrender to that which is unknown and unseen to the world.

Everyone has faith. Even the atheist has faith that there is no God. A hypochondriac has faith in sickness and disease. Those who fear something, have faith that whatever they fear can harm them. Whatever we truly believe about life and ourselves is where our faith is placed. There are two kinds of faith regarding religious or spiritual matters. One type of faith is based on the teachings of religious dogma. Many people accept, without question, what they are told by religious leaders. They have faith in what they are told. Most of these religions teach the principles of good and evil. If we do good deeds, we are rewarded in heaven. If we commit evil acts, we are punished in hell or some other place. Most of these religions teach that we are sinners who need to repent for our sins. These teachings are all fine and good in the sense that people learn certain values and many people find comfort in these principles. Young souls may be attracted to this type of teaching, but the religious teachings of these groups do not satisfy light worker souls who are seeking spiritual awakening while still in the body. Souls seeking spiritual enlightenment don't want to just believe in something, they want to know and experience the expansion of their soul. They want the faith of knowing and not just believing.

The faith that many religions promote is driven by the fear of hell. Fear is at the very core of this faith, because of the belief of burning in hell for all eternity. Some of you are aware of the Jonestown mass suicide in Guyana in 1978, during which 907 people committed suicide by drinking kool aid laced with poison. This event is symbolic of what is happening day by day in this world, in which the masses are constantly fed the poisonous news of the media. This constant bombardment of negative information makes us believe in a world of pain and separation. The only difference between the kool aid fed to the masses of people in the world and the kool aid that was taken in Guyana, is that physical death was brought on more quickly in Guyana. The kool aid that many religions and the media feed the masses of people every day is very slowly and insidiously poisoning our minds, until we are no longer able to think for ourselves. We then grow old and sick and seem to die, only to return to drink some more. The people in Jonestown had a strong worldly faith that Jim Jones, their leader, would lead them to a better life. Their belief in Jim Jones was strong, but they believed in a person who was just as lost as they were. The blind leading the blind can only result in becoming more lost in the darkness of this world.

How does a person acquire the faith that will lead to the awakening?

The journey of growing in faith may not be easy, just as metal has to go through the fire to be made stronger. We grow in strength and faith as we make the effort to let go of that which we know is not good for us and turn to that which leads to greater light. If spiritual awakening is truly the most important goal in our life, we will be presented with many opportunities to show our dedication to this purpose. Difficult experiences separate those who are ready for this spiritual journey from those who are not. I have known many on the path who when confronted with the difficulties of letting go of their old way of life could not take the heat and returned to their old life. This may have been exactly what the soul needed at the time so there is no judgment regarding their decision.

We cannot walk the spiritual path half-heartedly and expect much spiritual progress. Jeshua said, "Keep thy eye single and thy whole body shall be filled with light." Our total dedication to truth will transform our lives very rapidly. On the spiritual path we cannot serve two masters. It would be better for a person to put all his energy into gaining worldly riches than to half-heartedly seek the truth. The reason for this is that we are not going to make any spiritual progress doing it half way. Faith requires a total commitment. When a person begins the spiritual path in earnest, he begins to channel all his energy into his spiritual quest. This doesn't mean he has to stop participating in the world. It means that his desire for spiritual awakening must be at the center of everything he does.

Faith is not something we can touch, smell or feel but it is something that can be seen in the actions of those who are seeking enlightenment. When I first began my spiritual quest in this lifetime I did not have any proof that God existed, I just knew within that He did. I went through a lot of mental, emotional and physical hell without any outward proof that what I was going through would open the way to a greater connection with my Creator. I just had the faith and the willingness to endure an intense purification process without any outward assurance that anything good would come of it. I know that this faith was there because of my dedication and efforts in many past lifetimes of seeking to fulfill God's Will for me.

Let me try and explain this idea of faith through a story. Once upon a time, thousands of years ago, a large group of people lived on a very desolate mountain top. The terrain was very dry without any trees or water. The only water the inhabitants had available was the rare rain fall which only happened a few times a year. The mountain people dug a large hole in the middle of their mountain top to collect the rain water which provided small amounts of muddy water for the inhabitants throughout the year. Their food consisted of lizards and snakes which were not present in large enough numbers to feed all the people and so many of the people went to bed very hungry and some even starved to death.

The mountain on which they lived had no viable access to the ground below. All around the edges of the mountain top were very steep cliffs which dropped straight down thousands of feet to the valley below. Because of the cliffs on all sides, the mountain people were unable to get off the mountain. Another peculiar thing about the mountain they lived on was that from one side of the mountain you could look across an abyss of about 25 feet to a land full of abundance with fruit trees, beautiful clear rivers and abundant wild life. The people of the mountain tried for many years to figure out a way to bridge the abyss, but since there were no trees or anything else on their mountain top from which to make a bridge, they could only dream of being on the other side. Many had tried to make the leap of 25 feet only to fall to their death thousands of feet below. One man believed that if someone really prepared himself with a lot of practice, that the leap of 25 feet could be accomplished. He had a son whom he had been training to make this leap since the boy was 5 years old. The son was now 22 years old and had made several leaps on the ground that measured just over 23 feet but he had not been able to get close to the 25 foot marker. One day after a strenuous day of practice, the son was resting in his room when he had a very beautiful vision of himself making the attempt to jump the abyss. He saw himself in the air when all of a sudden a strong gust of wind helped to carry him across to the other side. The vision was so real and clear that the son knew that he would be able to make the jump. The son told his father that he was not going to practice anymore and that he would be making the jump soon. The father was very concerned because he knew his son had not yet made a jump long enough to take him to the other side. The son told his father not to worry and that all would be taken care of.

Several weeks later the son woke up one morning and knew that this was the day he was to make the jump. All the people of the mountain gathered in great anticipation and hope, because they knew that if one person could make it across, he could create a bridge which would allow all to cross over. The great moment had arrived for the son to make this daring leap. He knew that he would die if he allowed fear or doubt to enter his consciousness. He remembered his vision and had total confidence that he would make it. His whole focus was on providing a bridge for all the mountain people to have a much greater and abundant life. With this in mind, he summoned all his strength and determination and started his run toward the edge of the cliff. He used the edge of the cliff as a spring board and leapt towards the other side. While in the air, he felt a strong gush of wind behind him lifting him higher and pushing him further until he landed safely on the other side. The mountain people cheered in great joy for they now knew that that their lives would be completely changed for the better. The son immediately started making rope from the many vines that were growing on the other side. He tied a rock to the end of the rope and threw it across to the other side. He did this many times until he and the people on the other side were able to make a strong and sturdy bridge across the abyss. When the bridge was completed, all the mountain people walked across the abyss to a joyous, abundant life and lived happily ever after.

Now let me ask you a question. If the son had not practiced and prepared himself, do you think he would have had the faith to make the jump even after having the vision? It is through our efforts and willingness that we reach a place where our faith develops more fully and allows us to move through the limitations we have believed in for so long.

As our faith continues to grow, we will no longer have to be content with believing in God, we will know that God exists because we will have contacted God within our very being. Be patient with yourself as you travel this spiritual journey. You are a God being and your will is all powerful. This state of awareness may be a ways down the road but this is a truth that in time all souls will come to know. Jeshua said that he came to earth for those who had ears to hear and had the faith to follow him. Faith is having the courage to surrender to something that is not of this world. It takes a great deal of faith to go through all tests and hardships that the world of illusion places in front of us as we walk the spiritual path.

Faith in God, which is the same thing as faith in our true Self, is a virtue that comes from an inner attunement to our spiritual nature. Our degree of faith is dependent on our connection to God and how much we nurture that connection. Absolute faith is not faith in God, but rather the faith of God. Meditation and contemplation can be of great help in strengthening our faith.

It is difficult for this world to accept the idea of unlimited faith, because the mind of the world, ruled by the ego, believes in limitation. Limitation cannot and does not exist in the infinite Mind of God. We are part of Gods' Mind. It is interesting that the most fundamental of all truths is unknown to the great majority of souls in this world. The truth which I am referring to is the <u>knowledge of who we are.</u> This whole matter would be rather humorous if it were not for the fact that the great majority of people have so much faith in illusion and the pain that it causes.

There comes a point in a person's spiritual development when his faith has developed to such a degree that he may no longer need a spiritual teacher. This is in no way meant to dishonor a true teacher or his teachings. In fact it is honoring the teacher by fully accepting what the teacher has taught, which is that each one of us is a part of God. True spiritual teachers have come to earth to show us the way home. Ultimately the path that leads us home can only be found within ourselves. These great beings were the light and the examples that gave us the faith and vision to follow this truth. We are not accepting their teachings until we start accepting the fact that we too are the Way, the Truth, and the Light. They came to remind us of who we are. This is why a spiritual seeker, at a certain point in their growth, must stop being a seeker by relying on others and start accepting the fact that the truth is within their own being. In the beginning and middle stages of spiritual growth a person will benefit tremendously by having a true spiritual teacher, but there will come a time when he must accept his own divinity. Many spiritual aspirants will stay with their teacher until their awakening. Others may be guided to go out on their own, once their faith is strong enough. One who is guided to go on his own will still receive all the help he needs on his spiritual journey but at this stage much of the help will come from the spiritual realms.

I have been around a few spiritual teachers in my life and I received a great deal of grace and light from these beings. There came a point in my spiritual journey when I was directed to follow my own inner guidance. A spiritual teacher is an amazing manifestation of grace and we honor them by having the faith to surrender our illusions and accept what they are teaching. As long as we look to the teacher as having all the answers, we are not looking within ourselves which is where the truth exists for each of us. Don't get me wrong, we all need a lot of help and guidance until we are spiritually mature enough to follow our own inner light. The trap that many spiritual seekers fall into is the continuous reliance on the spiritual teacher for all their spiritual answers. It is sort of like a baby who does not want to leave the comfort and support of his mother. The baby definitely needs the time with his mother to gain the necessary nutrients, strength and knowledge before he goes out on his own. This does not necessarily mean that all ties are broken with the teacher. It just means that he has accepted his own inner light as his teacher. It is also very important not to leave the nest too early. If we're meant to travel the spiritual path on our own, we will be made aware of it at the appropriate time.

I remember very clearly when the time for leaving the spiritual nest was sort of pushed on me. After I left the Holy Order of MANS, which I mentioned in earlier chapters, I became involved in another spiritual group for a number of years. The head of this group is a very highly evolved spiritual being. My partner Linda and I had gone to see her in New York at an ashram there. One day during our stay, Linda and I were walking through one of the dormitories when we suddenly saw our teacher walking around the corner. Linda was acknowledged as usual by our teacher, but the teacher gave me a look which was cold and sharp. It was not the usual look of love, at least not in the way I had grown accustom to, but rather a hard look. She also did not say a word to me but engaged my girlfriend in a friendly conversation. It really disturbed me as I thought I had done something wrong.

Later, I was actually indignant and felt that there was no reason for her to reject me as I felt she had done. I had no idea at the time that I was actually being pushed out of the nest. My gut feeling about what happened is that our teacher recognized that it was time for me to go out on my own, but at the time I saw it as a rejection. My ego was having all sorts of resistance to the fact that it had not been acknowledged. It wasn't until a month or two later that I became aware of what that look was saying to me. It was at that point of being pushed out of the nest that I began my spiritual pursuit on my own. It was also at this time that my spiritual realizations took a quantum leap forward. I started to have very deep and profound experiences of who I am. Now I cannot say with full assurance that this is what my teacher intended with her look, but I know that everything happens for a reason and the result of this interaction was a change in my path and an acceleration of my spiritual development.

Jeshua said, "If you have faith the size of a mustard seed, you can say to this mountain, be moved into the sea and it would be done and there would be nothing that would be impossible to you." Jeshua did not say this to make his teachings sound lofty, he was stating an absolute truth. Jeshua not only knew the truth, he manifested it through his healings and so called miracles. His works seemed to be miraculous to others, but Jeshua was simply showing us that we have control over matter and not the other way around. This of course requires absolute faith.

Most people in this world are lost at this time because they belive in the lie of the ego. Through the power of spiritual faith we start to take control of the effects by understanding and changing the causes. Until we have the understanding that we and we alone are the creators of everything that happens to us, we will continue to be victims in life. Faith does not allow us to have a victim mentality. A person without faith will continue to see injustice, hatred and cruelty in life and her experiences will reflect that state of mind.

There is a saying: 'The intellect can lead you to the door of spiritual realization but cannot enter in itself'. In other words, we can talk about spiritual truths and contemplate the meaning of these truths, but the logical mind does not have the capability of grasping truths which are not of this world. We need to use the logical mind to start our journey, but it is not intended to take us all the way. The logical mind can be likened to a booster rocket on a space shuttle. Its job is to lift the shuttle to a certain altitude and then it drops away. The booster rocket was not intended to take the rocket ship all the way. The intellectual mind can carry us so far on our spiritual journey but it is faith which will carry us all the way home.

The word faith can seem very mystical or mysterious, but when we break it down to its basic component, we will find that faith is nothing more than acceptance. I will give an illustration which should make this idea a little clearer. Suppose a very large city was running short of water because of the high demand and the scarcity of rain. High in the mountains a few miles from the city, there is an enormous lake hundreds of miles long and wide and thousands of feet deep. The water in this lake is very pure and does not even need processing to drink it. The City Council decides to run a pipe directly from this lake to different parts of the city. The first pipe that was constructed was a foot in diameter and could not supply enough water to ease the burden of the city. The second pipe was two feet in diameter but still could not supply enough water which was needed in the city. The third pipe was ten feet in diameter and was able to handle all the needs of the city.

The main difference in the pipes was the size and capacity, or looked at in another way, the pipes ability to accept water. The more water the pipe could accept, the more it was able to fill the needs of the people in the city. In the same way, the greater the faith of an individual the more he will be able to channel the light, love, and power of God into this world. A meditation I had many years ago will help to clarify what I have just written. In the meditation I was shown the mind of the world and how God could only give people that which they could accept and how so many people accepted limitation, so that was all they could receive.

Along with our spiritual development and faith, the physical body must also be prepared. The body is the vehicle through which the pure energy of God is brought into the world, just as the pipes were the vehicle through which the water was brought into the city. If the pipes were all rusty and dirty with many holes in them, much or all of the water would be lost on the way down to the city. Even the water that reached the city through these pipes would be polluted. If our bodies are not prepared to handle the higher spiritual frequencies, we will not be able to channel much spiritual energy through them. The preparation of the physical body goes hand in hand with our mental and emotional preparation, because the body takes on the frequency of the thoughts, feelings and especially the beliefs that we have. If our mind and emotions are continually focused on the truth, then this focus will naturally begin to refine the body's vibration so that it becomes a purer receptacle of the greater light which can then be radiated into the physical dimension.

We must become more conscious of what we eat and drink as well as the need to exercise regularly in order that our bodies can accommodate the higher frequencies. It is our desire to know the truth which gives us the strength to prepare our minds and bodies as instruments of God here on earth. Faith leads to spiritual maturity and the awareness of our oneness with God. The most important thing is not whether we are a ten foot pipe or a one foot pipe, what matters most is that we have the faith to choose light over darkness, truth over illusion. The Holy Spirit will then be able to use us to the full extent of our abilities.

One morning, many years ago, I was asleep in bed and I thought I heard the alarm go off. I was sleeping and yet in my sleep I was wondering if it was time to get up. Still dreaming, I looked at the clock and saw the time, but I still wasn't quite sure whether I was dreaming or not. A few seconds later I woke up and then I knew absolutely what time it was and what I had to do. There's a vast difference between vaguely knowing something when you are sleeping and knowing that same thing when you're awake. When you're asleep, you may not be quite sure if what you are seeing is real or not. When you wake up there is no longer any question as to what is real or not. It is through our faith that we are able to walk the path which will eventually reveal to us the difference between being asleep and being awake. The difference between being spiritually asleep and waking up spiritually is the greatest difference a person can experience on this plane of existence. That is why a complete reversal of thought is needed because spiritual knowledge is the exact opposite of the beliefs of the sleeping masses. When we awaken spiritually, we will realize that we are infinitely more than we could ever begin to imagine with our intellectual mind.

I would like to grow in faith, but what if I don't have access to a spiritual teacher to help me?

A person seeking truth will always have access to a spiritual teacher, although the teacher may not always be in a physical body. You may have heard the statement: 'When the student is ready, the teacher will appear'. Interestingly the opposite is also true, 'When the teacher is ready, the students will appear'. In most cases, when a spiritual student is ready for deeper understanding, she will be led to a teacher in this world. The most important step in acquiring faith is our willingness to surrender everything we think we know so that we can open up to a totally new way of being. A spiritual teacher can help us in the surrender process, but if we are not led to a spiritual teacher in this world, there is a reason for that. There are many ways that the realizations of truth may come to us. Each of us is very unique and our needs are also very unique. Every person who is sincerely seeking truth will receive exactly what she needs for her spiritual development. Some students may be prepared by a teacher, or teachers, who work from behind the veil of illusion.

How do we know what we need in the way of a teacher?

Look around you and observe the situations and events of your life. If you are sincere in your desire to know truth, your life will contain exactly what you need to aid you in your search. If you are seeking truth, you will find truth all around you. It may be in the form of a spiritual teacher, it may come to you in the form of a book, it may be through your associations with others who are also seeking truth, or it may be through your own spiritual insights. Life will also reflect truth in ordinary, mundane situations. Some of our greatest teachings come in the form of difficulties and pain. Many times it is our most difficult experiences which cause us to look for answers that the world cannot provide. Don't sell these situations short just because they don't seem to be spiritual. In a TV series call the X-Files there was a saying, 'The truth is out there'. In our spiritual journey, we will find that the truth is all around us if we have eyes to see.

Everything and every situation in the life of a sincere seeker can be used for the purpose of helping in their awakening. Unfortunately pain, on one level or another, is part of the awakening process. We are voluntarily dying to our ego, to which we have given much life and power and so dying to this identity is not an easy thing to do. This requires tremendous faith. The renunciation of our ego identification is not for the faint of heart. As I said before, this voluntary relinquishment of the ego is symbolic of the crucifixion, which leads to the resurrection. Keep the faith and everything you need will be provided to you.

Some people think that they need to be at a spiritual retreat somewhere in the mountains in order to awaken more quickly. The thing we need to realize is that wherever we are is our own spiritual retreat. The kingdom of heaven is within us and if we are truly seeking the truth, everything is our life can be used to aid us in this process. We have the power within us, if we have the faith and the will.

At certain stages of our spiritual journey, we seem to test our faith by creating difficult scenarios in our life. This is all part of the spiritual process. This testing does not come from God as so many think. Why would God choose to test us when He has always seen us as nothing less than perfect? What would there be to test? We go through these tests as a way of revealing to ourselves just how far along the path we have come, or how much control the ego still has over our life. The spiritual path is a process of dissolving the unbalanced ego, the individuality we have clung to and protected all our lives. The ego does not go away without a lot of screaming, protesting and pain. It will do everything in its power to prevent us from discovering our true nature. This is where our faith is needed to transcend our ego.

Many times on our spiritual journey we will have to step out in faith to do things we don't want to do or don't think we have the ability to do. These times can be scary but if we have the faith that all things will be taken care of and that we will be able to accomplish whatever it is we are being guided to do, we will experience a fulfillment and joy which only comes through trusting in God.

Here's another story I made up to depict the process of acquiring faith. Once there was a young man named Eric who lived in a beautiful city near the highest mountain in the country. No person had ever climbed to the top of the mountain because of the treacherous slopes and the very high altitude. Many people had tried, but no one had even reached within a thousand feet of the summit. The people living near the mountain thought it was evil because several people had lost their lives in an effort to reach the summit. Therefore the mountain was named Diablo, after the devil. The summit of the mountain was considered impossible to reach. The best climbers in the world had tried in vain and so nobody had even made an attempt to climb the mountain in the past 5 years.

Eric loved mountain climbing and he dreamed that someday he would be able to conquer Diablo and reach the summit. Every day after work, Eric would go through the most grueling, strenuous exercises you could imagine to build his strength and endurance. He also practiced climbing different mountains during his weekend breaks, always choosing to climb up the mountains from the most difficult angles. After several years of preparation Eric felt he was ready to make his attempt to reach the summit of Diablo. He now believed he could conquer Mt. Diablo.

It was a beautiful spring day in early June when Eric set out for Diablo with his gear packed on a donkey. Upon reaching the base of the mountain, Eric set-up camp for the night. Early the next morning he began his ascent. On the first day of summer, June 21, Eric reached the highest point of the mountain that any climber had yet reached. He was now ready to climb the last 1100 feet without any knowledge of what to expect. Slowly he began his climb up sheer walls of ice, never knowing if the ice would give way which would mean certain death. Deep in his heart Eric believed he could make it. As Eric ascended the final summit, he began having difficulty breathing because of the altitude. He had also taken a couple of nasty falls, but fortunately was not injured badly. Many thoughts of giving up the quest entered his mind but each time he kept focused on just taking the next step. 'One step at a time' became his mantra. On June the 23rd, twenty one days after he began his climb of Diablo, Eric reached the summit of the mountain. He had transcended all the limited beliefs that the summit of Diablo could not be reached. He had done it.

Shortly after Eric had accomplished what had previously been perceived as an impossible feat, several other climbers were also able to reach the summit. Eric had broken through the limited belief that it could not be done and had opened the door for others to also reach the summit. In the same way, every soul who transcends the limitations of the world makes it much easier for those who are to follow.

In the beginning Eric dreamed about climbing all the way to the summit. After all his preparations and training, he then had the faith that he could do it. The final stage was his actual accomplishment. The different stages he passed through were from imagining, to believing, to accomplishment. Our faith is also developed in similar stages as we act and think in accordance with what we believe to be true. Eric didn't just dream about climbing Diablo, he did everything he could to prepare himself in the best way he knew. Training to climb a difficult mountain is not easy and takes a tremendous amount of dedication and hard work. Climbing the spiritual mountain is also not easy but the rewards are fulfilling in a way which no other path could bring.

Let us keep the faith by being persistent in our efforts. There is not one iota of effort that we expend on our spiritual journey that is not acknowledged by the Holy Spirit. Through the life of Jeshua and other great saints, we were shown what is possible. No matter what you are going through in your life, keep the faith. There are numerous beings on the higher planes who are aiding you in this journey. The grace and light that is now infusing the earth is blessing all souls who are making the effort towards greater conscious expansion.

CHAPTER 10

The Inner Child and Innocence

To regain our innocence there are two major factors that we need to address. They are both dealing with the healing of our inner child. The first factor is our birth into the world and the environment we are born into. Just being born into a body and having the feeling of being confined after being in a realm that is so loving and unlimited is a tremendous shock to the soul. Then we are subjected to the pain that our parents carry and to the environment we are born into. The pain that our parents carry is unconsciously passed unto us. This begins a process of disconnecting with our inner child and the loss of our innocence. The first seven years are critical in forming a child's foundation. Depending on the severity of the pain that we are exposed to during this time determines how badly wounded our inner child becomes. This wounded child within us must be healed if we are to become whole. We all know that having a strong foundation is very important when building a house. Without a strong foundation the house or structure could be severely damaged or even collapse during a strong storm. Without the healing of our inner child, we too are subject to a loss of balance when we experience a situation which activates the pain of our inner child. We also need to heal our inner child to fully develop into the amazing spiritual beings that we are.

What is the best way to heal our inner child?

It is through the power of our awareness or consciousness that this healing takes place. We first have to be aware that our deepest pains usually come from our unhealed inner child and not from what seems to be happening in the outer world. We then have to be willing to observe this pain without any judgment or interpretation. This observation is much more powerful when done at the time that the pain is consciously present. This process of being conscious of the pain without trying to do anything about it is extremely important in the healing of our inner child. We can look at our consciousness as a very powerful flashlight. By shining the powerful light of our consciousness unto the pain we start to dissipate the power of the pain. This may have to be done many, many times before a deep wound can be fully healed. This process is an extremely important part of our spiritual development. As we consciously observe this pain we may get an insight as to its origin which helps us understand the cause. This is not necessary, but it is helpful.

I had a very wounded inner child because of the loss of my mom and being put into an orphanage at the age of four. I can't even begin to count the number of times that I experienced deep pain because of situations that affected my inner child. I didn't know why until later in life why I was so emotionally affected by certain situations. Many times I would become very emotional when saying goodbye to women. I didn't even know some of these women very well and yet it affected me very deeply. I later realized that these situations were a reenacting in my mind of the loss of my mom.

After I realized what the major cause of my pain was, I began to practice the observation of this pain. I can't begin to count the number of times that I sat in my meditation chair to observe the pain that I was experiencing because of my inner child. This pain arose not just because of the loss of my mom, but also because of the treatment in the orphanage. There were times that the darkness and emotional pain was so intense that I felt like getting out of my meditation chair and running out the door. Many times during this process of observing the pain of my inner child, I would get feelings or insights as to the cause of the pain, but again this is not necessary to heal the pain. It is extremely beneficial to sit in silence and observe the emotional pain whenever it comes up or as often as you can. We are only able to connect with the great light that we are when we are willing to face the darkness within us.

The second factor is the deepest pain of all and that is the memory within our soul of the separation from God. This second factor is usually experienced as a soul reaches a high level of spiritual development. A therapist who was helping me to heal my inner child told me to go home to try and get in touch with the pain that I experienced as a child because of the loss of my mom. She wanted me to experience this pain because I was not allowed to as a child in the orphanage. So when I got home I went to my meditation room and sat and tried to get in touch with that pain. I was able to experience the pain to a certain degree and a few tears flowed down my cheeks. Then all of a sudden without even thinking about it, I got in touch with the pain inside me dealing with my separation from God. I had not even tried to do this but the experience was so powerful that tears just poured out of my eyes and I cried like I had never cried before. This went on for about 30 minutes. Even though I had tried to get in touch with my childhood pain, my soul was ready to deal with the deepest pain of all and it happened automatically. The seeming separation from God was our first experience of the loss of our innocence.

When most people hear the word innocence, the first association that comes to their mind is a very young child. Young children are, for the most part, seen as pure and untainted, in other words innocent. One passage in the New Testament describes a time when Jeshua was teaching and some children wanted to be near him, but the disciples tried to keep the children away. Jeshua told the disciples not to turn the children away because their very nature reflected those in the kingdom of heaven.

What do you think Jeshua meant by that? Does it mean when we finally enter the kingdom of heaven we will be as children? In one way this is true. As we regain the innocent nature we had as a child, we begin to experience the sense of wonderment and timelessness that we had as children. I mentioned in an earlier chapter that spiritual maturity and innocence were synonymous. This means that we will not only regain our innocent nature, but we will be able to experience the joys of innocence with a fully developed mind. The innocence in children that Jeshua was referring to is a mind that does not know of evil, time, and separation. In this state of innocence, every moment is totally new and boredom is impossible. Unfortunately in our day and age, children are exposed to so much negative information so early in their lives that it doesn't take long for them to lose their childhood innocence.

I remember when I was a child how everything was so new and exciting to me. The colors were so much more vibrant and alive. Everything was happening in the present moment and I wasn't concerned with the past or the future. I didn't have the greatest of childhoods, but during that innocent period, everything was a mystery which opened up a whole new world of possibilities. I remember playing with the wind and chasing butterflies with total abandonment, freedom, and joy.

Most of us remember the period of time when we believed in Santa Clause. Wasn't it a joy as a child to believe in someone so magical with his flying reindeer? As a child I would run out to the yard on Christmas day to see if I could find the reindeer prints in the snow. Even in the orphanage the spirit of Christmas was alive as we waited in great anticipation for Christmas Eve and Christmas Day. In the orphanage, we were usually only given one present for Christmas, but what we were given was cherished. One year I got a toy car which would wind up as I pushed the wheels against the floor and then I would let it go and it moved across the floor with lights flashing. It was a real treasure to me. As I write about it I get a very clear picture of that time and feeling. If physical childhood innocence can bring such joy from something so insignificant, just imagine what we have in store for us as perfectly innocent spirits in God's unlimited kingdom.

I also remember when I started to lose my innocence and entered into the world of time and fear. In the orphanage, the nun who was in charge of us kids was a very sadistic person. If we did anything that she considered wrong, no matter how innocent it was, she would take us aside and beat us with a piece of 2 x 4. We would have to pull our pants down and lay over a bed while she would hit us with all her might on our butt. It was very painful and we were not allowed to make a sound while we were being beaten. We would receive anywhere from 10 to 100 whacks depending on the mood of the nun. Anyway this nun would often make me wait the whole day before beating me, which meant that during that day I dreaded the arrival of evening when I would receive the beating. It was during this time that I became familiar with the concept of time as I anxiously waited for the boom to be lowered. I clearly remember the anxiety I felt during those days. I dreaded the waiting almost more than the beating, but the worst part was losing that childlike innocence.

Later in life as I entered my spiritual journey I realized why I had chosen to experience such a traumatic childhood. I realized the nun was only playing out a part in my dream, as I was playing out a part in her dream. It would be foolish of me to blame her for the trauma I went through, because if it had not been her it would have been somebody else. I chose to go through that experience for a certain reason. To judge the nun as being at fault would entangle me in that karma, rather than freeing me. Forgiveness of our self and others is the only path of liberation from any painful experience.

We are probably all familiar with the story of Adam and Eve in the Garden of Eden. In this story Adam and Eve were told that they could eat of any tree in the garden except for one tree in the very center of the garden. They were told that if they ate of the tree of the knowledge of good and evil they would surely die. A serpent then came along and tempted Eve telling her that she would not die if she ate of the tree, but that she would become as God. Now the fruit of the tree in the center of the garden was very tempting, so Eve ate of the fruit and gave some to Adam to eat also. The story goes on to say that when they ate the apple, their eyes were opened and they saw that they were naked and so they hid themselves. The story states that God then cast Adam and Eve out of the garden because of their disobedience.

The story of Adam and Eve is taken very literal by many religious groups, but the symbolism of the story reveals a much deeper understanding of what happened. I will not go into detail of what all the symbols mean, but I want to give you an overall picture of the true meaning of the story of Adam and Eve and how this relates to the loss of our innocence. Adam and Eve represent the souls who decided to journey into the darkness of creation. Only a small percentage of all souls made this journey into darkness which caused a deep sleep to fall upon them. In the darkness, the souls seemed to fragment into many parts or individuals. Many souls are dreaming similar experiences as ours in different worlds and different realities. Our focus for now is on this world, which is the densest plane of illusion for a soul to enter.

Adam and Eve were very innocent while they were in the Garden of Eden. The Garden represents our conscious unity with God and the unlimited love, joy and innocence which are our natural state. While in this state of innocence, there was no concept of good and evil. The concept of separation and time were also non-existent in this state. Remember we were created in the image of God, in fact we were made from God's own Consciousness. We each had our own unique awareness of what was taking place.

The souls were created in perfect balance, with each soul containing both positive and negative polarities. The positive polarity is considered a male energy, whereas the negative polarity is considered female. The positive polarity was more outgoing and mental, whereas the negative polarity was more receptive and feeling. The serpent tempted the negative polarity of the soul telling her that she would be as God if she ate of the tree of the knowledge of good and evil. The serpent represents the first appearance of the false ego which lured us into illusion. The ego caused certain souls to question why they were the created and God the Creator. This intruder into heaven convinced the soul that it could create a place outside of God where it could be the creator and take the place of God. In this dark, illusory state, the ego was free to be in charge. Now remember the false ego is not a real thing, but is rather an illusionary concept consisting of false beliefs, desires and above all, guilt. The ego succeeded in tempting the soul to create an unreal state in which the ego could now live out its lie. The ego's existence is totally dependent on us experiencing and believing that the separation from God is real. All evil and darkness are the result of the illusionary ego.

How is it possible that something like the ego could come into existence in the perfect Mind of God?

It is not really possible and that is why I keep saying that this is all a dream. This world is no more real than a fleeting thought that arises and disappears in your mind. As I said before, don't spend too much time thinking about it because it can be very confusing. The time will come when our conscious expansion has reached a point where enough of our inner light is illuminating our mind and will allow us to see through the illusion and we will be free.

Ever since our self-eviction from the Garden of Eden, we have been trying to regain our positive/negative balance so that we might return. This is why men and women seek each other for relationships, hoping that the relationship will bring the balance and joy that we lost a long time ago. The true balance is within each soul, as each one of us, in our true nature, is a perfect balance of female and male polarities. The mystical marriage between the two polarities will take place when divine wisdom and perfect love unite in the soul. Don't worry about losing the intimacy with others, because when we awaken, we will have a closer and deeper intimacy with others than we ever thought possible. We are one!

One very interesting teaching in A Course in Miracles is the idea that we shall enter heaven two by two. It's interesting when we look at this through the filter of Noah and his Ark. Noah was told to collect two of each species to place on the ark. A Course in Miracles refers to spiritual coupling as a Holy Relationship. A relationship based on need and desire is referred to as a special relationship. In the special relationship, each partner is trying to get something from the other to make himself feel whole. This will never happen in such a relationship, because special relationships are based on a need which can only be filled from within each individual.

In the Holy Relationship, there is an understanding by the two souls, that soul expansion is their goal. In the Holy Relationship, there is an effort by both parties to see the other as being perfectly innocent and divine. Through acknowledging the divinity of their partner, both of them are awakened. So in the Holy Relationship the other is our savior as we are theirs. We can have this Holy Relationship with everyone we meet. We can practice superimposing over their physical appearance the spiritual reality of who they really are. As we do this our vision adapts to see ourselves in the same light.

Let me use another story I have made up to try and paint a clearer picture of the Adam and Eve saga. Once there was a beautiful kingdom far up in the mountains. The king and queen of the kingdom were very loving and wise and the subjects of the kingdom loved them very much. The mountain on which the kingdom was built was filled with beautiful trees and flowers of all varieties. The animals in the forests were completely tame and they loved to play with the children of the kingdom. The weather was absolutely perfect all year round and the crops were always very abundant. The water which ran down from the highest peaks of the mountains and filled the reservoirs of the kingdom had a magical quality to it. As a result of drinking the water there was no death or disease in the kingdom. People would grow to whatever age they desired and their bodies would then cease to age. Life in the kingdom was a paradise.

One day a very great event took place, one that all in the kingdom had looked forward to for some time. To the great joy of the king and all the subjects of the kingdom, the queen gave birth to identical twins named Mary and Michael. The celebration in the kingdom was without precedent and lasted for three months.

The children grew in grace and their lives were filled with joy, beauty, and love. Fourteen years passed and the children were now old enough to officially take their positions as prince and princess of the kingdom. This included the authority, responsibility and honor that went with those positions.

One day, shortly after their fourteenth birthday, the prince and princess were out riding by themselves when a beautiful young man appeared to the princess. The prince was riding a little ahead so he did not see the man. The princess was intrigued with the beauty and presence of the man and the wisdom that seemed to emanate from him. The man told the princess that she and her brother were not being treated fairly by the king. The princess did not understand what he meant, so the man explained that because the king and queen will never die that she and her brother would never have the opportunity to become the king and queen they deserved to be. The princess told the man that she was very happy as a princess, but the man told her that the power and glory that come with being a queen is even much greater. The princess thought for a while and then asked the man what she could do. "All you have to do" the man said, "is renounce your father and mother three times and I will make you king and queen of a kingdom much greater than this." The princess was now very excited at the prospect of being a queen, so she did what the man said and renounced her parents three times. She then called her brother and told him to do the same so that they could be king and queen of a greater kingdom. The brother did the same and as soon as he renounced his parents, the two of them were immediately transported off the mountain to a very arid and hostile land far below their parents' kingdom.

The prince and princess were somewhat disturbed by this new land. They could still see their parent's kingdom far away in the mountains, but there was now a huge chasm between the land they were now standing on and the kingdom. The two children now felt a little remorse, but the idea that the man had put into their heads of being king and queen was very strong and they went about searching for subjects to govern. Instead of finding willing subjects, the prince and princess encountered hostility from others who were also looking to create a kingdom for themselves. It wasn't long before the prince and princess realized that setting up their own kingdom wasn't going to be as easy as they thought. They now had to put most of their efforts into simply surviving in this hostile land.

Life became more and more difficult in this strange land. The joy and freedom they experienced in their parents kingdom was replaced with feelings of pain and sadness. Soon they were arguing with each other and blaming the other for getting them into this mess. After much arguing they realized they could no longer live together and decided to go their separate ways. It didn't take very long before they both started to experience a great deal of loneliness and so they went searching for another to fill the emptiness they were feeling.

After many years and much suffering, the prince and princess accepted the fact that they had made a terrible mistake and longed to return to their parents' kingdom. The only problem was the huge chasm between their worlds. How were they to bridge such a large gap?

I'll end this story now, because this is the state in which many people on this earth find themselves at present. There is a huge gap between heaven and earth, but there have been many great souls who have created bridges between the two. Every soul who awakens makes it that much easier for those who are to follow. I especially honor the life of Jeshua Ben Joseph because at the time he was born the karma and darkness on the earth was so strong that the earth was heading into a place of darkness from which it might not have been able return. Through his willingness to go through the crucifixion, he was able to release enough of the earth's karma that the direction of the earth was altered and started ascending into the light. I can hear some thinking, 'Here's another Christian who thinks the only way is through Jesus Christ'. I am not saying that a person must believe in, or follow Jeshua in order to return home. There have been many other great saints who have also sacrificed their lives and created bridges between heaven and earth. Any true spiritual teacher can lead others across the bridge. Jeshua and the other great saints don't care if you acknowledge what they did, they only care that you return. It can be through the path of Buddhism, Judaism, or any other path that will lead you home. I can tell you that I understand what Jeshua accomplished through his life here on earth and I am eternally grateful for the path he has opened up to us.

The story of Adam and Eve states that once they ate of the apple their eyes were opened. It would be more accurate to say that after eating the apple their eyes were closed. The eyes that were opened were the illusory physical eyes which perceive life through the vision of duality and separation. This distorted vision was the beginning of struggle and pain.

Our technology has evolved to the point that a person with poor eyesight can have their vision corrected with a laser procedure. The truth is that regardless of how great a person sees physically, he is still blind if he has not had his spiritual vision opened. We've probably all been in a car where the windows have been iced over on a cold night. Without defrosting the windows it is impossible to see clearly out the windows. Our vision is so obstructed by the ice that it would be very dangerous to drive without the windows being defrosted. The spiritual asleep individual is like somebody driving with their windows all iced over. He will bump into so many things and often have a bad accident. If we use only our physical vision then we will continue to walk through life blindly. We will not really know what to do and which direction to take. Our spiritual sight allows us to see through the illusion of the physical world.

The ego is so cunning that it can take on the role of the spiritual aspirant if we are not fully aware of our motivations. This is why the virtue of innocence is so very necessary. I mentioned in an earlier chapter the practice of 'impersonal self-observation'. We might ask ourselves what is our motivation for our spiritual striving. Is it for self-glorification and recognition, which only strengthens the ego? Or is it for our sincere desire to serve others and to regain our union with God? If we are not careful, the ego can convince us that our spiritual striving is a very selfless endeavor, when it really is just another method through which the ego glorifies its existence. Innocence does not recognize any difference between our self and others. Spiritual innocence acts out of love and union, because the true nature of innocence is to see and accept all things as one.

It is a strange state that we have created for ourselves, in which we have an easier time accepting the idea that we are guilty, rather than accepting the truth of our innocence. Contemplate the truth, repeat affirmations based on spiritual truths, practice seeing the truth wherever you are and the darkness will slowly dissipate, revealing a most beautiful sunrise.

Most of us have watched a moth flying around a flame. The moth is very attracted to the flame, but if it gets too close it is immediately consumed by the flame. Our spiritual desire is what attracts us to the divine flame of love, but our ego tries to frighten us by telling us that we will die if we get too close. In a sense the ego is correct in that everything which is false within us will die and we will be reborn into a state of perfect innocence and joy.

It is very difficult not to love an innocent child, unless the darkness in a person is so thick that very little light is shining in their minds. You've heard the saying that charity begins at home. Begin by loving yourself and accepting the pure innocence of your being. You are deserving of everything, without any limits. Everything you deserve is permeated with pure and perfect love. You deserve everything because you are and always have been perfectly innocent in your oneness with God. Find your innocence by seeing it in others.

Throughout this book I have been speaking of the need to completely transform our way of thinking, but don't make the mistake of being hard on yourself. One of my greatest lessons was learning how to let go and relax and not feel I had to attain perfection immediately. I had an ascetic attitude for a good portion of my spiritual journey. We should be easy on ourselves, love ourselves and allow others to love us also. We have done nothing for which we should feel guilty or ashamed. We simply need to understand the truth. Discipline may be beneficial for a short time in order to gain a spiritual foundation, but at a certain point of our spiritual journey we need to focus on the fact that we are and always have been innocent and thus honor ourselves.

Our understanding and living according to truth is the path to our awakening. Even before we complete this journey, we will begin to feel the joy, peace, love and light fill our life. This will make it so much easier to let go even more fully. Be a happy face. Renounce all ideas that God desires sacrifice, because that is the opposite of truth. Observe happy young children at play and that will give us some idea as to the attitude we should seek to emulate. As we accept the fact that we are perfectly innocent we will make room for much more joy.

CHAPTER 11

Letting Go

One of the first teachings I received in the Holy Order of Mans was to 'let go and let God'. This is a very simple phrase, but there is an infinite depth to it when the meaning is fully realized. Many of us are so used to trying to control our lives, that it takes a great deal of faith to fully turn over the direction of our lives to God. It is in times of trials and dealing with obstacles that we find out if we are really willing to release the steering wheel to God. During Jeshua's ministry people would come up to him with problems about different facets of their lives. Jeshua told them to look at the flowers in the field and how there was no effort on their part and yet they unfolded in all their beauty and splendor. He told the people that if the flowers of the field, which are only temporary manifestations of the beauty of nature, are taken care of then how much more will God take care of you who are eternal children of God.

Having the trust to let go and accept that our needs will be taken care of requires that we have a connection to our heart. It is in being connected with our heart that we begin to allow the flow of creation to manifest in our lives. It cannot be done with the mind alone. The mind is normally dealing with our exterior life whereas the heart is dealing with our inner reality and our connection to the Divine. Our connection with our heart opens the way for creation to flow through us and empower us so that we can fulfill the purpose for which we entered the earth realm. There is a perfect flow in creation which we can connect with by attuning ourselves with our heart. This flow of creation is sort of like a powerful stream of life that fills all creation. The heart is the conduit through which it enters the physical realm. There is no limit to this powerful flow and there is no limit to a soul who has fully connected with his sacred heart. This is why it is so important to get in touch with our heart. The heart is our connection between the spirit and the physical.

The heart is a most amazing organ and it is a most sacred and holy place through which we can contact and connect with God. Even though it seems that it is our brain through which we respond to life, it is the heart which is the true director of our journey through life if we allow it to be. Through quantum physics and our advanced technology, it has been discovered that the heart is the true brain of the body. The world has been led to believe that it is the brain which directs all functions in the body, but that is not true. The heart directs the brain and the brain then transmits those directions to the body. The field of energy that the heart produces is many times greater than that which the brain creates and thus exerts a greater influence on all our bodies. Once a person reaches a certain level of spiritual development, he will begin to be guided by the Heart. The heart is the sanctuary where God dwells and in meditation we can make contact with the Creator through our heart. When you enter meditation, focus on your heart. Allow the heart to guide you in all areas of your life.

Years ago in meditation, I was automatically guided to focus on the heart and breathe very rapidly into this most sacred place. My breath was very strong and without effort. The feelings that were coming from my heart during this time were very beautiful. This automatic breath into my heart went on for many months. I was not sure exactly what was happening but I sensed that the heart was being attuned and energized by the powerful rapid breath work that was taking place almost automatically. At this time my meditations are almost always totally focused on my heart.

133

Letting go and letting God is an act of great faith. Many times a person has to reach the bottom before they realize that there has to be a better way. It is at this point that many turn to God and ask for help, not knowing how help is going to manifest. They have come to a point of surrendering. The last thing the ego wants to do is relinquish control and thus the stage is set for the spiritual aspirant's inner battle with the ego he has created. This is the most difficult part of our spiritual journey. It is stage three of our journey which I spoke about in an earlier chapter.

As I have noted earlier in the book, a large portion of my spiritual journey in this lifetime was very difficult and painful. The last few years of my journey were interspersed with times of peace and times of intense changes going on within me. It was as if I were on a boat traveling down a wide river with occasional strong rapids. I had no idea where the river was taking me, I simply let go of all expectations. I had opened the doorway to my heart and had surrendered completely. I actually experienced faster growth during the times the boat was going through the rapids. Inwardly I knew that everything was happening in perfect synchronicity and in perfect harmony with the Will of God. I didn't have to do anything, except simply be and do whatever was placed in front of me. I was fully aware that even the difficulties I encountered were a gift which allowed me to let go of even deeper layers of pain and false beliefs.

There comes a time in a person's spiritual development where she realizes that there is nothing she needs to do in order to awaken. More than that, she recognizes that as long as she feels she has to do something to awaken, she will keep the awakening at a distance. As long as we believe that this world and all its pain is something real that needs to be escaped, then we are accepting the illusion as reality.

You keep telling us that we need to act and think in a certain way in order to free ourselves from this illusion and now you are telling us that we don't have to do anything. Exactly what is it that we are to do?

I mentioned that a person has to be at a certain stage in their spiritual development for this idea to be used as a guide to live by. If a person has not reached this stage of spiritual development, then this idea would not be appropriate, nor would it be helpful to the individual.

In the beginning and middle stages of the spiritual journey a lot of spiritual, mental, emotional and physical preparation is absolutely necessary, but there will come a time when the spiritual seeker is no longer a seeker. As long as we are seeking something, we have not yet found it. A state of knowing must be reached before the seeking ends. At this point a person does not have to do anything except to be in the present moment. Whatever the present moment brings is accepted fully without any resistance, knowing that whatever is taking place in that moment is exactly what is needed for her greater awakening. She has reached a level of faith in which she knows that she is taken care of completely. She knows that even though she has not fully awakened spiritually, that all things needed for her awakening automatically appear in her life without any effort on her part. She has reached a state in which she knows that she can do nothing of herself and so she has completely let go allowing God to direct her life.

Something that is extremely important to understand for anyone on this path is that their first and foremost duty is to heal themselves first. Many on this path want to help others before they themselves have been healed. They mean good, but we really can't help anyone spiritually unless we are actively healing ourselves. Once we are healed we automatically radiate the light and love to those around us who are open to receive it. Honoring ourselves is extremely important. Shakespeare in one of his sonnets touched on this idea when he wrote, "This above all, to thine own self be true." I again want to repeat that our highest purpose for coming into the world is to heal ourselves.

As we walk on this journey we will be used in a way which is perfectly suited for us. God has a plan for each of us in this process of awakening that the world is currently going through. It is as if all light workers are each a piece of a giant puzzle. We all have our particular place and purpose in this puzzle. The puzzle cannot be completed until each one of us has fulfilled our part. Jeshua said, that a candle is not lit to be put under the bed or under a bushel, but rather it is placed where it can give light to the entire house. An awakened person will be guided to be exactly where he is supposed to be. He will be placed in a situation which will allow the light within him to influence the souls he was intended to contact. The awakened ones are kind and compassionate. Some may appear to be very unconventional. The one thing that is different about these souls is that they know that none of this is real and so there is nothing to struggle against. It is their awareness of the truth which sets them apart, even though most people would not be able to tell them apart from the masses.

The spiritual path is intended to awaken us to who we are. An exercise to help us remember who we are is as follows: close your eyes and allow the mind to cease all thinking. It may take a little while, but wait until your mind is completely still. Now with the mind very still with no thoughts, notice that you are still aware. This awareness, void of all thoughts and identifications, is a state which can help lead you to the awareness of who you truly are.

In the beginning of our spiritual journey, it takes a tremendous effort of will to swim against the current of the mass mind of this world. The belief system of the world forms a strong current in which many younger souls are swept along. Many people are not aware enough, or strong enough to begin this upstream journey. As we sincerely travel this spiritual journey we will be given access to the strength needed to transcend the world. We will not lose anything that is real, only that which is an illusion. That which is real can never be lost.

How would one go about swimming against this current, or mass consciousness?

A person must first want the truth above all else before he can begin the process of waking up from this dream. Understanding truth reveals that the beliefs and thinking of the mass mind of the world are perpetuating an illusionary existence. Truth will reveal to us who we really are and what we are not. This realization automatically puts us on a different path which is in the opposite direction of the mass mind of this world.

Many believe that the crucifixion of Jeshua has saved them and all they have to do is believe this and they are free. So they blindly follow the dictates of the religious group they are involved in without questioning what the true purpose of Jeshua's life was about. These people believe and follow their leaders, who in some cases are as asleep as their followers. Jeshua did clear a lot of the karma of the world through his crucifixion. This made it a lot easier to see the light, but each one of us has to make the decision and effort to seek and become the light ourselves. Finding that light requires letting go of the desires of the world that cover up the light. As I said before, it doesn't mean we become an ascetic, it means putting the truth first. The truth is not that complicated. The question is how much do we want it?

When I joined the Order, I met my first teacher, Father Paul, who told us about a student who came to him one day and complained that he felt like he didn't know anything. Father Paul replied, "Ah, so you finally got it." He was informing the student that by letting go of everything he thought he knew, he was making room for the truth to enter. Father Paul continually taught that we must become zeros for Christ.

Our spiritual journey in this world is a process in which we battle an illusionary foe. After many battles, we finally realize that the foe we were fighting against was our own belief system. At that stage we understand the words of Jeshua when he said, "Resist not evil." By no longer resisting, we completely give up our self-efforts and allow God to bring us to the final step of full spiritual awakening. This is a long process of self-effort and finally letting go so that God can complete the process. Let your heart be your guide and you can never go wrong. At some point we will find it very amusing that we have been fighting against something which does not exist in order to gain everything that exists eternally.

Becoming nothing in the world has nothing to do with our material assets or position in the world. As I have shared many times, the transformation and the resurrection all take place in our mind, or more accurately in our heart. It is in the mind where all the work is done but it is in our heart where we experience our union with God.

In truth, separation from God is an absolute impossibility because God is all that is. Where could we possibly go to separate ourselves from God? We need to be very vigilant any time the slightest disturbance arises in our mind or body, because these little upsets allow us the opportunity to free ourselves more fully. Whenever I experienced any kind of emotional upset, I would take time and observe the emotion without any judgment. I found that by giving it attention without any judgment or interpretation, the effect of the emotion would lessen. The pain of my inner child was my biggest teacher in this lifetime.

The spiritually awakened individuals have great compassion for the world. They know of the hardships and suffering going on in the world, but in order to help others out of this nightmare, they must stand on the rock of truth. They cannot lend validity to the illusion by seeing it as true and blaming and judging others for what is happening. It also doesn't mean they condone what the terrorist seemed to have done. They recognize the dream for what it is and at the same time provide any help they can to others according to how they are guided. A spiritually awakened being has compassion for both the victim and the perpetrator without any judgment. When the Christ state is realized, there is no judgment against anyone because of the knowing that this is just a dream and that we all have been on both sides of the drama. We have been the terrorist as well as the victim. The Christ Consciousness has transcended both the darkness and the light with the knowing that they are two sides of a whole. You cannot have one without the other.

This next truth might be difficult for some to accept, but we and we alone have created the whole world we seem to be participating in. We and we alone are responsible for forgiving this whole world that we have created. As long as we project guilt on anyone or anything in the world we are in a sense projecting that guilt unto ourselves through our judgment. Only after we have forgiven our self completely for the judgments we have projected unto the world will we be able to reach a more expanded state of consciousness.

If I have created this world and everything in it and every other person in the world has created this world, then why aren't there billions of worlds?

There are seemingly an infinite number of physical worlds and realities created by the thoughts of souls in the physical dimension. Quantum physicists have discovered than any thought that was ever imagined, resulted in a world where that imagination could find expression. The quantum world with all the many dimensions, parallel universes and infinite possibilities are all very intriguing and fascinating, but they can distract a person from focusing on the present moment and the spiritual purpose of awakening. All knowledge that we need to further our spiritual advancement will be available to us each moment as we sincerely walk the spiritual path. Every one of us is responsible for the entire physical universe we seem to inhabit. We are all experiencing a totally different universe because of our different states of mind and what we believe. Our beliefs determine what is projected on the screen of our mind. Just notice how people react differently to headlines in the news. A person caught up in illusion will react very differently to a situation than one who is awake. An awake person will not react but will respond to a situation in the way in which he is led. Each of us has our unique perspective and experience of the world because of the fragmentation of the mind, which seemed to take place at the time of the separation. Therefore when an individual fully awakens spiritually, the fragmentation of the mind dissolves and he sees through the eyes of oneness.

Scientists say that the physical universe is over 15 billion years old. Are you saying they are all wrong?

Well for one thing, time does not really exist, but in this dream world of linear time we could say that it has been going on for that long. We shouldn't be concerned with time but instead put our efforts into focusing on the present moment. The statement that there is nothing new under the sun is correct. The past, present and the future have already come and gone. It all happened in less than the blink of an eye. That is why this whole physical universe will disappear in the awareness of a person when he awakens.

Most people have heard of the idea of living in the Now. Now let me give you a spiritual gem which can really help you in breaking free of illusion. **The most important thing you will ever do is what you are doing at this very moment.** If you can perceive the value of this statement you will have a very powerful practice which will dramatically speed up your spiritual progress.

Are you saying that if I am tying my shoes, I must look at it as the most important thing I have ever done?

You're missing the subtle point I have made. Let me ask you a question. Is there anything you can do outside of this present moment?

No, not really.

So if there is nothing we can do outside of Now, wouldn't you say that Now is all we have? If Now is all we have, shouldn't we give everything we have to this very special eternal moment? The future and the past are just that, so the only time we have is this current moment. Time is one of the biggest illusions of all. We can speed up the process of awakening immensely by practicing being in the present moment. I mentioned before that the ego cannot exist outside the illusionary realm of time. The ego needs our belief and involvement in time to exist. Living in the Now is a very powerful spiritual practice.

We all have to make plans for future events and we need to learn from past events. So why should we let go of time?

When you make plans for the so called future, are you making those plans in the present moment, or are you making the plans in some future time? The answer is obvious that you can only make plans for the future Now. Are the lessons you have learned in the past helping you in the present or are they helping you in the past or future? I am not being facetious when I say these things. I just want to impress upon you that the present moment is all we will ever have. The current moment contains everything we could possibly desire for our fulfillment, because God dwells in the timeless state of Now. Letting go of time and being in the present moment is an extremely important spiritual practice.

The problem that the vast majority of people have is that a great deal of their physical, emotional and mental energy is tied up in the past or the future. Very little of their energy is left to use in the only time there is, which is Now. To answer your previous question, a person who has awakened does more for the spiritual freedom of mankind when he is tying his shoes, than a politician signing a treaty for world peace.

That is a very difficult idea to accept. How can an insignificant act such as tying our shoes be more important than peace in the world?

Because in the great majority of cases, the politician signing the treaty is still functioning in a dream world in which good and evil, peace and war are believed to be real. He is working in the realm of effects and is trying to change an effect with an effect. This is absolutely impossible. It would be like a person in a movie theater yelling at a character on the screen who is about to be attacked by a lion. He can yell all he wants, but it will not change one iota of what the outcome of the movie will be. How can something that isn't real be fixed? As long as a person believes in the world of appearances, he will be stuck in time and illusion. He will continue to dream that evil exists and if he believes himself to be a good person, he will do what he can to try and eliminate it.

Don't get me wrong, we should all do our part in trying to make this world a more peaceful and loving place to live, by spreading good will to everybody we meet. A person who has awakened from the realm of time is spreading the light of truth just by his very presence. Whether he is tying his shoes or giving a lecture, the light in him will continue to shine forth and be a healing presence to the mind of the world.

Jesus came into the world to change the world. Are you saying he was working on a false premise?

Jeshua and other great spiritual beings came into the world to bring the light of truth into the world and not so much to change the structure. Jeshua said, "Render unto Caesar what is Caesar's and unto God what is God's." These great beings came to awaken those who were ready to move on in their spiritual evolution. The mistake the church and other religious institutions have made is that they have made these spiritual beings special and different from the average person. That is not at all what these great beings came to teach. They came to show us that we too are the way, the truth and the light. They came to shatter the false beliefs and illusion of this world. The light they brought is like a great seed that was planted in the earth. This seed has now grown into a great tree of light which is now encompassing and giving light to the whole world. The light which they brought into the world has made it so much easier to understand the truth. Jeshua said he was in the world but not of it. The great spiritual beings knew this world was not real, but because we believed in this illusion they came to plant the seed of light so that we might wake up from this nightmare.

The point I'm making is that a spiritually awake person is doing more for the healing and betterment of the world than 10,000 politicians who are writing policies to try and make the world a safer place to live.

Let me give you another analogy to help make this idea a little clearer. Imagine that several billion people were trapped in a very dark, immensely large building with no light and had no idea how to get out. They were afraid to take a step not knowing if some abyss lay before them. A group of 10,000 political leaders were in charge of coming up with a plan to help the people out of the dark building, but since they were living in the same darkness as the others, they were of no help to the masses. They came up with many plans and theories, but nothing seemed to change the fact that people were trapped in the dark. In fact, things seemed to get worse in the dark building. Now imagine that unbeknownst to these people, each one of them had an unlit candle on their person. Some even talked about the mysterious candle but did nothing to light it, or teach others to light it. So the 10,000 leaders sat around discussing theories on how everyone might get out, but since nobody knew the way out, their theories meant nothing.

In far corners of the building a few people discovered their candles and learned how to light them. The light from these candles allowed people around them to see clearly enough to start moving toward the exit of the building. Who provided the greater assistance to the people trapped in the building, the 10,000 who had all kinds of theories on how to get out, or the few who actually provided light for others to see how to get out?

Trying to change things in the outer world without changing the inner, is like a person whose house is on fire and tries to fix it by rearranging all the furniture in the house. Of course this does nothing to address the cause. The fire keeps burning and destroying the house as the furniture is being moved around.

We've all probably seen professional magicians perform acts which seemed impossible, only to find out later that the trick was done with mirrors or some other gimmick. This is exactly what the ego has done to make this world seem real. It has done such a great job that the whole world has swallowed the ego's **lie,** hook, line and sinker. One tool that all magicians use is distraction. They distract the audience by doing something with the right hand, while the left hand can manipulate something in order to make it appear magical. The ego has set up everything in this world as a way of distracting us from the truth. These distractions can be anything from money, fame, disease, pain and death. The ego will create any circumstance in order to keep us believing that this world is real. Even though the ego seems to be a good magician, we must remember that it was us who seemingly gave life to the ego and it is us who, through our own inner light, will be able to let go of our identification with the ego.

A truly great magician is a spiritual magician who helps others to free themselves from the deadly magic of the ego. The awakened person knows the ego's tricks and how to expose them. As long as there is an audience which seeks to wake up, the true spiritual magicians will appear from time to time to help people free themselves from the illusion of the ego.

The advancement of our technology allows us to experience virtual tours which seem so real. Our technology is becoming so advanced that when a person experiences the virtual effects, it is as if the person is actually having the experience. If you contemplate the idea of how real some of these virtual experiences seem to be, it might help you to gain some insight into the illusion of this world.

Many have to reach a spiritual crisis before they are ready to let go and let God. We need to reach a state of mind in which we realize that we really don't know what anything in this world is for, or what it represents. When a person finally comes to the realization that he really does not know anything, including who he is or what this world is all about, he will have reached a state of readiness to fully receive the truth. We must become as nothing to attain everything. God has given us everything and the ego has given us the illusion of pain and separation. Which one are we going to choose?

How can we function in this world if we let go of all we believe?

You will function in a much more efficient way than you ever thought possible and it will be without any effort at all. As we get our unbalanced egos out of the way and let go, we allow the Power, Intelligence and Love of God to flow through us. Talk about maximum efficiency, this is it. These truths cannot be experienced through words, but words can be a road map to the destination I have been talking about.

CHAPTER 12

Our Journey Into and out of Illusion

Shortly after I was ordained a priest in 1971, I had a meditation in which I was shown that there were two types of beings on the earth. One type came down to earth from above and the other was a native to the earth. I had an idea of what the meditation meant at the time, but it wasn't crystal clear until I came across a web site which contained a number of channelings from Jeshua on a number of subjects. There are many people in the world who claim to channel Jeshua and many are true channelings. Before accepting the information coming through the channelings, feel what resonates with you. If it resonates with you, then this may be information very beneficial for you. If not, simply move on. The information I am referring to was channeled through Pamela Kribbe, a woman living in the Netherlands, who has been channeling Jeshua for many years. I knew the information coming through her channelings was from Jeshua the first time I heard it, as it resonated with me right to my core. One idea which runs through many of these channelings clarified the meaning of my meditation.

I will now state in a very condensed version, in my own words, the essence of what Jeshua said regarding the idea of two types of beings on earth at this time. If you want the full picture, I would highly recommend going to the web site 'www.jeshua.net' to get the full story. When I was led to this site, I immediately downloaded all the audio information that was available on the Jeshua channelings and put it on CDs and my iPod and listened to it over and over again. It is a veritable treasure of spiritual information for all light workers.

In the channelings, Jeshua stated that when God created the cosmos, Her creation was a reflection of Her nature which is all good. Her goodness and light permeated all that was, but after eons of time She realized that there was something missing. As strange as this may sound, His creation lacked the aliveness which comes through the dynamic of opposites, it had become static. God, being all good, could not create that which He was not. To give you a better idea of this state, think of a world pervaded by love with an abundance of wealth where everybody has everything they could ever want without working for it and no one ever dies. From the day a child is born in this world, he is showered with love and the abundance of everything he could imagine. Do you think that the people of this world could really appreciate, or even recognize, what love or abundance is? They would have nothing to compare it with and so after eons of time there would be a sense of stasis in which everything is always the same. Eventually, even this beautiful, abundant world would be missing something. This is a very simple explanation of what happened in heaven. So God came up with a way out of this conundrum. He came up with the idea of forgetfulness or ignorance. Ignorance, or the idea of forgetting who we are, was the key to getting God's creation un-stuck.

God asked a certain group of very courageous souls to take the plunge into illusion and duality, into a state in which they would eventually forget who they were. In the beginning of this plunge there was still a remembrance of our union with God. Slowly but surely this connection was forgotten as we sank deeper and deeper into darkness. We not only lost our connection with God, but we started to forget who we were. We experienced the state of separation from God for the first time ever. This was extremely painful for the soul. This state of forgetfulness was needed in order to accomplish the task at hand. In forgetfulness of who we were, we could then experience duality. Duality contained the opposites that were needed to bring about a new state of consciousness in the souls participating in this adventure. This new state of consciousness is the Christ Consciousness which Jeshua first displayed when he walked the earth over 2,000 years ago. God knew that this new consciousness would bring greater aliveness and dynamic into His creation once these souls returned to heaven. The souls who volunteered for this sacred mission were to create this new consciousness by experiencing both the darkness and the light in a physical body. Eventually after many cycles of time and after experiencing both suffering and joy, the souls would reach a state in which they would be able to encompass and transcend the opposite states of good and evil. Does this not sound a little like eating of the tree of the knowledge of good and evil? This is sort of like completing the circuit through which energy can flow by having both a positive and negative polarity.

Jeshua speaks of souls being born in waves. The souls who volunteered to enter into illusion were from the first wave of souls ever created. These souls are referred to as 'light workers' by Jeshua. After these souls took the plunge into illusion and fell asleep, they eventually came under the spell of the ego or individuality. This was not a bad thing, but was rather part of the process of understanding the opposite of light, which is darkness. The ego promotes power as a most treasured prize and so the desire for power created conflict amongst the souls who had entered the illusion. There were inter-galactic wars during that time which lasted a very long time.

While the inter-galactic wars were taking place, the earth was created as an experiment by having many different kinds of life forms existing on one sphere. Jeshua states that many of these different life forms on earth, beginning with one celled organisms, were inhabited by a new wave of souls who were, in a sense, in their infant stage. Many light workers took part in the creation of the earth souls. As the forms of life on earth became more and more evolved, eventually the human body emerged. It was actually the desires of the earth souls to experience different life forms which brought about this whole evolutionary process on earth. When the earth souls, as

Jeshua refers to them, reached a certain point of development, the galactic beings took great interest in what was happening on earth. They thought of a way they could use the earth souls in their battle for dominance. They interfered with the development of the earth souls by manipulating their consciousness and DNA in order to use them for the purpose of battling their enemies. The galactic beings did not respect the soul quality of the humans, but were only seeking a way of using them to accomplish their own goals.

There are many stories in written and picture form from many ancient civilizations about higher beings coming down to earth. These beings were looked upon as Gods by the earth souls. Even the bible refers to a time when the Sons of God came down and mingled with the daughters of men. These are all references to when the older galactic souls visited the earth for different purposes.

Now, I will get back to the meaning of my meditation. A time came when the galactic beings became tired of fighting because it had lost its luster. They had reached a point in which they were now ready to begin their move out of the ego stage and into the next stage before their re-awakening and entering into Christ Consciousness. This is the stage in which the heart becomes the primary motivator of the soul. The galactic beings realized the wrong they had done to the earth souls and wanted to make amends. At some point, many of these older souls decided to take on human bodies on earth so that they could bring light into the earth to help the earth souls and make up for how they had mistreated them. Thus they are called light workers. The Jeshua channelings very clearly revealed the meaning of my meditation in which I was shown that there were two types of beings on the earth at this time, the light worker souls and the earth souls. At the time of the descent of the light workers into physical bodies, the earth souls were not yet ready for the help and information the light workers were trying to impart and many light workers were persecuted, tortured and killed for their efforts. Also, the ego was not fully under control in many of the light workers. With their sophisticated knowledge and lack of ego control, they caused upheavals on earth which resulted in the destruction of civilizations like Atlantis and Lemuria. Throughout many of the past centuries on earth, this play of the older souls wanting to help their younger brothers has been taking place. Many light worker souls have not yet awakened from the darkness and duality of earth and are suffering because of an inner knowing that the earth is not their home.

During this new age with the higher frequencies coming into the earth, there will be great opportunities for the light worker souls who are still asleep to begin waking up. Some younger souls are now also ready for this knowledge but most are still caught up in duality. This brings us to our current time in which a great transformation is taking place upon the earth. We are now in a time when a new heaven and a new earth are being created. All souls have been invited into this new paradise and each one of us will decide whether or not we choose to enter.

I have depicted the above story as briefly as I could, while still describing the essence of what transpired. For those who are interested in getting the full picture, I have already given the source location. Light workers have come in large numbers at this time of the earth's development to aid in the transformation that the earth is currently going through.

There are many earth souls that are not ready to leave their ego stage and they will not be able to survive on the new earth at this time because of the higher frequencies that are pouring into the earth. They will go to a place in which they may continue their journey in a realm which is more conducive to their state of consciousness. There is no judgment in this. Each soul is always in the perfect place and situation which they have created. Everyone has the perfect right to choose whatever path and experience they desire. All souls will eventually return to their oneness with God. Many souls may desire a greater experience of darkness to accelerate their own soul development which is a courageous act on their part.

The light workers who came here to help, but have not yet awakened may give you some idea of the courage it took to voluntarily enter illusion. The earth is the most difficult and dense planet in creation for a soul to experience and yet it serves as the greatest opportunity for soul development.

In a parable in the New Testament gospel of Matthew, Jeshua refers to the Christ Consciousness as the pearl of great price. "The kingdom of heaven is like unto a merchantman seeking goodly pearls, who when he had found one pearl of great price, went and sold all that he had and bought it."

In the Jeshua channelings he likens the search for the Christ Consciousness to deep sea divers diving into the ocean again and again seeking the pearl of great price. Jeshua states that what is really taking place by diving into illusion again and again is that we are creating and becoming the pearl of great price through the very experiences of illusion. Eventually through our transcendence of the duality of good and evil the Christ Consciousness is created. To create the pearl of great price, the Christ Consciousness, we must learn not to judge, not to see darkness as bad but as the other half of light. This means being able to view all the atrocities being committed on earth without judgment but with compassion and a desire to help others in whatever way we are guided. It is a recognition that our purpose of coming to earth was to experience both the dark and the light. In this journey we have been the perpetrator as well as the victim. Our whole purpose of coming into duality was to learn about the darkness as well as the light, so there is no need to judge.

In the song 'The Impossible Dream' there is a line in it which very much depicts the light workers decent into illusion. The line in the song I am referring to is: **'To be willing to march into hell for a heavenly cause'**. That is literally what light workers are doing, only they do it many, many times until their mission is complete. By going through the darkness and eventually transcended it, we create a dynamic in heaven which had not existed before our journey into illusion. As painful and dark as the journey into illusion may seem, the more joyous and illuminating our return to heaven will be. There is a statement by Jeshua which was revealed to us in the Holy Order of Mans in which he said: "He who sees the greater darkness, will see the greater Light."

Interestingly there is a similarity in the creation of a pearl by an oyster and the creation of the Christ Consciousness by souls. An oyster creates a pearl because of an irritant which has entered its' inner shell and the oyster starts to build a barrier around the irritant to protect itself. The barrier eventually becomes a beautiful pearl. We entered into duality which caused a great disturbance to the soul by encountering darkness. The light worker souls had only known light up to this point. Through countless experiences of pain and darkness, we grew in wisdom and grace and learned to understand, encompass and transcend duality. The Christ Consciousness is the greatest gift that a soul can give to its Creator. Everyone reading these words has created, or is in the process of creating, this priceless pearl. This sacred path is honored and celebrated by all the angelic and heavenly realms. We are truly blessed and we should honor ourselves for the great purpose we have taken on by entering into duality. Through this understanding we must also realize that there is never a need to judge anyone or anything.

Because of the great pain and darkness we experience here on earth, many may question the compassion of God by asking us to enter into duality. What we have to realize is that **we are God.** Each and every one of us is a spark, an individuation of the great reality known as God.

Jeshua stated that one of the traps that many light workers have fallen into is trying to help those who have not asked for their help. I'm not so much talking about helping them in regards to their physical situations. I'm talking about trying to help them spiritually before they are willing or ready to enter the spiritual journey. A soul is a law unto itself in regards to choosing what path he wants to take. God gave us free will in the beginning and will do nothing to retract this gift. We and we alone determine what we are to experience. As I stated before, a soul may want to descend into greater darkness to fully experience that state before choosing to return home. There is no judgment or condemnation from God, only compassion and love. If we want to complete our purpose here, we also should observe the actions of others with compassion and love, for they are the ones who will eventually have to experience the results of their own creations.

Trying to help someone spiritually before they want it, is like trying to help a butterfly out of a cocoon before its time. The butterfly gains the strength needed to survive in the world by using its own strength to break free from

GILBERT ANDRES ESQUIBEL

the cocoon. If the butterfly is helped out of the cocoon by another force, it will not have acquired the strength needed to survive and will die shortly after its emergence.

We gain our strength in duality by encountering numerous experiences of darkness and light. Through these experiences, we slowly begin to remember who we are. As the knowledge of who we are continues to grow, our perception of how we look at life changes dramatically. Remember, we see what we believe and we become what we see. Growing on our spiritual journey is like constantly changing glasses. Our vision is constantly expanding as our understanding grows. What we thought was true a year or even a few months ago may not be true for us today. The more spiritual light we have, the clearer everything becomes. When we have become fully developed spiritually, our vision is infinite. In that state of development, whatever we need to see or know is shown to us instantly.

As light workers, we need to be very aware of the information that is entering our consciousness. Watching the worldly news, reading newspapers and following political happenings can be likened to taking poison if we are not yet fully grounded in our spiritual knowing. The delusion of the mass mind of this earth fills the airways and newspapers and if we're not alert, this information will pollute our minds. Our minds are like computers which are constantly being programmed by the beliefs and experiences we are exposed to, so we need to be discerning in what we allow into our reality. Years ago, I found that I had to stop watching political programs as I constantly found myself getting agitated. Politics is the epitome of duality.

In just about all spiritual material there is the mention of our oneness with God, which I also have mentioned many times in this book. Through the findings of quantum physics and our scientific development, we can now relate this idea of our oneness with God in a scientific way. Quantum physics has discovered that any part of a holographic projection, which is called a fractal, contains all the information of the whole, just as a cell in our body contains all the information in it to make a new body. If we were to take an atom from just one cell of our body, that atom would contain all the information to make a whole new body. We could keep breaking each smaller piece of the whole into smaller and smaller pieces and would never come to an end. Each piece, no matter how small, would contain all elements and structure of the whole and this would go on into infinity. Each piece, no matter how small, would be a reflection of the whole. We are an extension of God.

Quantum physics has also found that all the power and energy needed to recreate the big bang is contained in a space the size of a proton, the nucleus of an atom. This is an infinitesimally small amount of space and yet it contains the power to recreate the entire physical universe. Most Light Workers accept that each one of us is a part of God and eventually we will be able to accept the fact that we have all the attributes and power of God. The truth is that we are all part of the unimaginable and glorious holographic reality of God. When we can fully accept this truth, we will remember who we are.

God is infinite in every way and as a part of God we too are infinite. God always was and always will be without beginning and without end. As God creates through thought and desire, so do we. There are an infinite number of possible realities we could experience according to our desires. Most large modern malls have movie theaters with many choices of movies to view according to what we want to see. In the same way, we determine what kind of life we choose to experience, although there is another factor that must be taken into consideration in these choices and that is karma.

It is hard to conceive of God not having a beginning and yet there must have been a time when God decided to create us and everything else that exists.

When I consciously started my spiritual journey in this lifetime, I spent hours trying to conceive of the infinite idea of God in a finite way that I could grasp. I wanted to package up the concept of God in a way that my finite mind could comprehend. This was not possible and I gave myself some headaches trying to do this. It's like trying to contain the oceans of the world in a teaspoon.

Man is so used to thinking in terms of time, space and boundaries that it is very difficult to describe ideas that are outside the realm of time. Think of God as One Universal Mind which is infinite in every way. Within this One Mind, all that ever was and ever will be is taking place. If we conceive of God in these terms, we may begin to understand that time and limitation could have no reality in this great Mind. This One Mind and Spirit always existed. It is the very essence of life and awareness. Within this Eternal Oneness, there was an event which took placed in which God decided to create us as companions, with all the attributes and power of Himself/Herself. So in one sense there was a time when we came into being. On the other hand we were always there as a possibility. Since there is no time and no beginning or end, I will ask you to contemplate this question and come up with your own answer.

When we came into being we were one with God and were given free will. Without free will, we could not be true companions to God. It was through this power of free will that we chose to enter illusion. This decision seemed to create the illusionary universe that we seem to be dwelling in.

All is One in God and yet in this Oneness, there is relationship. This is another conundrum that the intellectual mind will not be able to fully experience. We are greater and more powerful that we could ever imagine with the intellectual mind. This terrifies the ego because the ego can only exist in limitation. That is why a person who is very strongly identified with his ego is terrified of the light of truth. As I stated before, light is the darkness most feared by the ego.

We journeyed into illusion and became trapped for some time. We escape illusion by the creating of a new consciousness. I would now like to expound a little on the state of Christ Consciousness. As with most virtues, there are different degrees of attainment. Most people when they hear the word Christ Consciousness would think of Jeshua or Buddha, someone who could perform miracles. Christ Consciousness in its beginning stages is a state in which one does not judge anyone or anything. It is a state of consciousness which sees good and bad, light and dark as two sides of the same coin. The Christ Consciousness has compassion for the victim and the perpetrator. She knows that she has experienced both roles many times. The Christ state is also a state of non-resistance. There is absolutely no resistance to anything that happens because there is a knowing that everything that happens is exactly as it should be. The Christ Consciousness knows the purpose and benefits of entering this illusionary state of duality and for taking on the roles of both good and evil.

One who has reached this beginning state of Christ Consciousness, even though it is not fully developed, has already performed the greatest of all miracles. He has created a new state of consciousness which had not existed before the appearance of Jeshua 2000 years ago. He has fulfilled the purpose for which man entered the earthly plane of existence. He has fulfilled Gods' purpose for the soul entering duality. That purpose is to experience, incorporate and eventually transcend light and dark, good and evil in order to create a new consciousness. She has created the Pearl of great price. In the creation of this pearl, she has completed her cycles of earthly existence, her karma is complete. She may choose to re-enter the earth again to help others who are seeking the light but this would be her choice. There are many individuals now on earth who have reached this state of Christ Consciousness and there are many more who are in the process of creating this consciousness.

The fully developed Christ Consciousness is a rarer state of consciousness at this time. It is a state of being in which he is literally manifesting God on earth. It is a state of being in which all power and knowledge is available to the individual. There are no limitations placed on this individual. An individual of this state of attainment usually comes to earth for a special purpose.

In closing this chapter, I again want to reiterate to light workers the extreme importance of learning to see good and evil, darkness and light without any judgment but as the two halves of one thing. Through this understanding and the transcendence of both, we fulfill our mission in duality by taking on the Christ Consciousness and expanding God's creation.

Conclusion

I have mentioned the mysterious word **truth** numerous times in this book. Before his crucifixion Jeshua was brought before Pontius Pilate who was the governor of Judaea at the time. Pilate knew of Jeshua's teachings and asked him, "What is truth?" Jeshua remained silent as he knew that Pilate would not be able to understand. A person will only know the truth when he has gone through the crucifixion of the ego and the resurrection of the Divinity within. Truth is always ready and waiting for a soul when he is ready to awaken. There are so many versions of truth in the different religious and philosophical arenas of the world. So what is truth? In a course of miracles Jeshua stated that Truth could be summed up in two words – **God Is**. In my meditation I was fully able to comprehend the great depth and reality in those two words. The truth truly is that simple when our minds are ready and clear and we have released the belief that we are guilty for some imagined sin.

Jeshua states in A Course of Miracles that the separation from God happened over millions of years and that before every soul experiences the full awakening, it will probably take at least that long, if not longer. In this illusionary realm of time we have free will and thus it is up to each soul as to how long he will take to let go of his individual ego and awaken to reality. It is up to each soul as to how much more pain and darkness he wants to experience before he begins his return home. Each soul will eventually get so tired of the pain and darkness that he will begin the journey which leads to the spiritual light.

I have created many analogies and stories in this book to reach different levels of awareness in those reading this book. I want to tell one more story to portray a clearer picture of our journey from our sleep state into the real world. Bob and Joan were amongst a large group of people who were in an airplane which had crashed in a very dense and dark jungle. Fortunately the denseness of the foliage in the jungle formed a cushion for the plane as it crashed. Nobody was killed, but many were injured. The pilot had gone off course and so nobody really knew where they were. As the people got off the plane, the first thing that really struck fear in their hearts was how dark it was. They knew that in clock time, it was around noon, but the denseness of the forest allowed only a very small amount of light to penetrate to ground level. The radio and all the instruments in the plane had been destroyed in the crash, so they were unable to put out a distress signal.

The people unloaded all the food, water and other supplies that would be needed, but they soon realized there would only be enough food and water for a few days. This caused even more fear among the crew and passengers. The pilot called a meeting of everyone. When all were assembled, he told them that one of the last readings on the planes instruments, before the crash, indicated that there was an ocean beach about 200 miles to the east of where they were. He said the beach was a launching area for large cruise ships taking people to beautiful vacation spots and that reaching the beach was their best hope of survival. The only problem was that because of the darkness in the forest, he had no idea which direction was east. The compass was broken during the crash so the only thing he could suggest was to pick a direction and start walking. He told them that because of the short supply of food and water that they would have to try and find water and food in the forest.

The pilot said that there were four flashlights on the plane, but without a compass there wasn't a guarantee that they wouldn't be traveling in circles. This caused a palpable panic among the passengers. The panic turned into arguments and even some fights. It seemed that the darkness was already taking its' toll. They couldn't agree which direction to take, so they decided to break up into four groups and each group would take one of the flashlights and travel in four separate directions. If one group reached the beach, they would notify the authorities to launch a search for the other groups.

After much soul searching and contemplation, Bob and Joan, who were both very spiritual, decided to go with the smallest group. Each group was given a certain amount of the supplies. The amount each group received was determined by the number of people in the group. The passengers were unaware of the presence of many different varieties of poisonous snakes in the jungle. After traveling for three days about one quarter of the group that Bob and Joan were in had been bitten by snakes and were suffering horribly. The medicines that were available seem to have no effect on the poison. It appeared that those bitten were doomed to die. It was almost impossible to see the snakes because of the lack of light. This created even more fear among the group. The fear caused arguments and the breaking up of the group. Bob and Joan were very distressed and didn't know what to do. Bob knew that Joan always had a very strong sense of intuition and so he asked her which direction they should take. Joan sat down in silence for some time before telling Bob that she felt they should go in a certain direction. Nobody else in the group was taking that direction so they were on their own.

Each day Joan would begin by contemplating the direction they should take before continuing their journey. They encountered some hardships along the way, but they also came across water holes and wild fruit trees which provided their needs to stay alive. Even though they felt very blessed and guided, Joan and Bob felt very discouraged. They didn't know how long they could avoid the snakes and if they were even going in the right direction. At one point they even talked about giving up and letting nature take its' course, but because of their spiritual foundation they summoned the strength to continue the journey.

Then one day the light appeared. They could now see very clearly that the direction they had been taking was leading them to a clearing. In fact, they could even hear the sound of the ocean. This brought tremendous joy to them and they continued the journey at an even faster pace. The next morning as they were heading into a clearing, they saw the most beautiful white sandy beach and ocean directly in front of them and ran towards it with all the strength they had left. When they reached the beach, they saw a beautiful large ocean liner docked a few hundred feet off the coast. There were a few people from the crew of the ship waiting for them on the beach with a boat to take them to the ship. Joan and Bob asked them how they knew they were coming, but the crew just smiled and welcomed them with much love. The couple told them about the other people lost in the jungle. The crew assured them that they were aware of the others and had sent members of the crew to help them out.

Joan and Bob were taken to the large ship, where they were given very beautiful accommodations. They were provided with new clothing and everything else they needed. After Joan and Bob were settled, they were introduced to everyone on board and soon discovered that many on board had, at one time or another, been lost in the same jungle and made their way out. The couple was then told that they would be taken to a very beautiful land across the ocean where all their questions would be answered. This land was a place so beautiful and joyful that it would be hard to describe in words. Once the couple had acclimated to their new home, they would be given the opportunity to join the crew in helping others out of the jungle, or staying in the new land and teaching newcomers as they were rescued from the jungle. Bob and Joan were assured that they would never again know pain, sadness or lack of love. They had returned to their real home.

I hope this story gives you a clearer picture of our process of waking up from this dream of illusion to enter a world of light and joy. The dense jungle represents the world of illusion where darkness reigns supreme. The poison snakes represent the ego who seeks to poison our minds through fear and guilt. Joan's intuitive faculty represents the voice of the Holy Spirit within each of us. The greater light coming through the trees is the beginning of our spiritual illumination. The crew from the ocean liner represents the spiritual masters and our spiritual guides who are constantly working with us. Of course, journeying to the new land represents our entrance into the new world.

I wrote about an experience I had at the beginning of my spiritual journey in this life, in which I was told to remain simple and I would reach my destination. The spiritual truth is very simple, but it is our identification with the ego which makes everything so complicated.

I want to end this book with some very simple statements which I have experienced and know to be true: We are perfectly pure and innocent and nothing can alter that truth no matter how bad we think we are. The truth is that we have never done anything wrong, we have fallen asleep spiritually and are having a bad dream. There is nothing to feel guilty about. It is through our intention and dedication that we will be given the understanding through which we can awaken from this dream. What we believe determines what we experience in life. One of the most important practices is that of forgiveness but we must remember that we are forgiving something which is not real. To reach the state of Christ Consciousness, which is the object of entering duality, we must let go of all judgment and accept all that is happening with non-resistance.

We are all unique and are all having very different life experiences. During different stages of our journey, one soul's truth may not be true for another. It is the intentions and dedication of a soul which determines what truth is for them. This is why I have written this book for light workers because all light workers have come into earth with the intention of remembering who they are and to aid the earth souls who are seeking the truth that will set them free. I truly honor and am grateful to all the light workers on the planet today and to those of the past. This journey through the darkness of this world is not an easy path to walk and light workers are celebrated by the ascended souls and angelic realm above. I know this path can be very difficult and sometimes it seems like we are not getting anywhere, but keep the faith for we are in a time when the doors to the higher realms are open wide for all of us. We are truly in an age in which we can make that final step of transcending duality.

CONCENTRATION EXERCISES

I will now give you a couple of concentration exercises that we practiced in the Holy Order of Mans. Any serious student on the spiritual path knows the extreme importance of having control of their thought process. One of the first exercises given to new students in the Order was the practice of concentration. Without the ability to concentrate, control of the mind is impossible. We also need to still our minds at will to successfully meditate. When we realize that our every thought is a creation in itself, we will understand why it is so important to know what goes on in our mind all the time.

I will now describe the first concentration exercise I practiced in the Holy Order of MANS. It consisted of taking an orange and placing it in front of me on a clear desk or table. Then, in my mind I would perceive the orange as our beautiful sun. This whole exercise is done in your imagination. I would then peel the orange and see that the segments of the orange are sort of like the twelve house of the zodiac. I then removed one of the segments and opened it up. I studied the consistency of the fruit and saw that the seed in the segment can be likened to a planet in our solar system. I then planted this seed in fertile ground and saw the spring rain nourish the ground. I then saw the seed in the ground sprouting and then slowly pushing up and breaking the surface. I then watched this sprout slowly going through the process of becoming a mature orange tree. I then saw the tree in spring bursting with orange blossoms. I then focused on one of these blossoms and visualized it going through the stages of becoming a beautiful, fully developed orange. I then picked the orange I had been following in my mind and superimpose it on the orange on my desk. This completed the concentration exercise. If you do the exercise correctly, it should take from seven to ten minutes. If at any time during this exercise you find your mind wandering, you should go back and start again. In the beginning we all had a hard time before we could consistently go through the exercise without our mind wandering. I was very vigilant in doing this exercise. In my first couple of years in the Order, I spent a lot of my extra time doing this exercise. I probably did the exercise three to six times a day for the first couple of years in the Order because I knew how important it was to quiet the mind so that my thoughts were in accord with what I desired to experience. After the first couple of years I practiced the exercise whenever I felt I was being carried away by my thoughts.

Another concentration exercise is to go to a quiet place in your house and light a candle. For five to ten minutes, stare at the flame without any thoughts interrupting your concentration on the flame. This is an exercise you can do any time you have a few spare minutes. I wish you all a most glorious journey on your way back to our oneness with God.

Printed in the United States
By Bookmasters